CAMPUS CRIME & SAFETY

SECOND EDITION

Christina Mancini, Ph.D.

Associate Professor of Criminal Justice
Virginia Commonwealth University
L. Douglas Wilder School of Government and Public Affairs

Kendall Hunt
publishing company

Cover image © Shutterstock.com

Kendall Hunt
publishing company

www.kendallhunt.com
Send all inquiries to:
4050 Westmark Drive
Dubuque, IA 52004-1840

Copyright © 2021, 2022 by Kendall Hunt Publishing Company

TEXT ISBN: 978-1-7924-9162-7
PAK ISBN: 978-1-7924-9164-1

Printed in the United States of America

Contents

Introduction to the Text

Nestled in the "ivory tower," college campuses tend to be safe environments for students, but crime and violence do occur. As explored in the first appearance of this book in 2015, crime trends vary based on the location of the campus (suburban, rural, urban, "college town") and their "type" (four-year universities, small liberal arts colleges, community colleges). Even so, there are certain classifications of crime that seem to plague colleges and universities in the U.S. The second edition of *Campus Crime and Safety* reviews the latest statistics concerning the nature and extent of offending that occurs in post-secondary institutions, efforts designed to prevent violence on campus, research-driven initiatives for preventing victimization during the college experience, and specific resources for campus crime victims. Given the turbulent year of 2020 and the ensuing social unrest and activism following the murder of George Floyd, particularly on college campuses, the second edition's focus is expanded to cover an additional "special topics" chapter exploring the role of student activism.

© Susan Montgomery/Shutterstock.com

The goal of the text is not simply academic in nature, but rather to ensure students and those who work in college settings are educated about the risks and dangers—albeit low—on campus. Criminal victimization brings with it many costs and hardships. Crime is associated with psychological, emotional, and financial problems. For this reason, becoming "crime savvy" is essential to ensuring the college experience is memorable for the right reasons. By the end of this text, readers will be better informed about crime on our nation's college campuses, how colleges and universities have responded to the crime problem, self-protective measures, current debates and discussions concerning free speech and the college campus, and the many victim resources available for college students.

Specifically, the second edition of this text is organized into five substantive chapters. Each of which explores the campus crime problem across different dimensions. The first chapter examines the nature and extent of crime, such as crime measurement systems and general prevalence trends and patterns of campus victimization. In another direction, the second chapter outlines general responses to crime on campus—including law enforcement efforts, the use of disciplinary review boards, federal legislation, new legislative responses, education, and victim-centered responses. By contrast, the third chapter summarizes research-driven initiatives for addressing crime on campus. Accordingly, three major criminological theories useful for understanding criminal victimization are applied to better understand crime patterns among college students; additionally, studies that have evaluated research-support policies for campus crime

© Tyler Olson/Shutterstock.com

prevention are summarized. In the wake of the turbulent year of 2020, Chapter 4 tackles a "special topic," entitled, "Social Unrest and the College Campus." The fifth and final chapter is designed to be a "how-to" for students and members of the university community who find themselves in need of information regarding the variety of resources available for victims and survivors of crime perpetrated on campus.

This text incorporates several pedagogical features designed to increase comprehension of major concepts and objectives. In particular, each section opens with "activate your thinking" questions that orient you to the upcoming material. A second feature, "learning goals" outline the specific aims of the chapter. These two features are particularly helpful for testing your retention after completing the chapter. In contrast, a "snapshot summary box" highlights and further explores a notable idea or concept. Throughout the text, "reflections" pose "real world" scenarios to readers. Because anyone can be a victim of a crime or play some role in preventing victimization, these questions aim to contextualize the material in light of everyday experiences.

It has been said that it takes a village to raise a child. The same could be said for completing a text! I am grateful to many talented and generous individuals. First and foremost, I extend my sincere gratitude to the Kendall Hunt Publishing team. Curtis Ross, Senior Acquisitions Editor, and I initially explored this idea in Spring 2014 and with his steadfast assistance, this text is now in its second edition! He is truly passionate about providing college students with the very best in instructional delivery. I am so very grateful for his help and faith in undertaking this project with me. Abby Davis and Paul Carty were also exemplary supports during the entire publishing process. I am thankful to have had their assistance. I would also like to acknowledge my colleagues in the Wilder School at Virginia Commonwealth University for their support. My students—both past and present—deserve tremendous gratitude and praise for challenging and impressing me on a daily basis. Finally, I thank my family—my favorite daughter-unicorn, Sasha Louise, and my superhero-husband Jesse for all of their love and support.

The Nature and Extent of Campus Crime

1

ACTIVATE YOUR THINKING

1. How do we measure campus crime in America?

2. What are the challenges of these strategies?

3. How much crime is there?

4. What factors are associated with campus crime?

LEARNING GOALS

- To compare and contrast the methods that exist to measure campus crime
- To critique crime measurement system
- To demonstrate the extent of campus crime
- To review patterns and trends of campus crime

At first glance, measuring crime, particularly those offenses committed against college students, might seem like a straightforward undertaking. The reality is it is much more complicated than simply calculating say the number of people arrested in any given year. Separately, institutions of higher learning have a stake in promoting the image of a safe collegiate environment. Moreover, many crimes, even serious and violent crimes committed against individuals, may not be officially reported to police. Indeed, crime measurement is so onerous that the federal government has enacted far-reaching legislation that requires transparency in the reporting of campus offenses across nearly all colleges and universities. This chapter further explores crime measurement issues by first reviewing the major crime data systems. It then moves toward identifying prevalence trends in student-involved crime and victimization over time. The chapter concludes by summarizing the major patterns of crime on colleges and universities. Beyond informing you about crime measurement, trends, and patterns, the chapter is useful for illustrating the crime problem in the U.S., particularly concerning its impact on college students.

Measuring Crime

Comprehending crime measurement is a critical step toward appreciating the nature and extent of crime in institutions of higher learning. Measuring crime is no easy endeavor. Generally, Uniform Crime Reports (UCR), one of the nation's leading methods of measuring crime in the U.S., represent official crimes reported to law enforcement (Federal Bureau of Investigation, 2021a). However, the UCR does not provide information regarding where exactly a crime occurred (e.g., a university parking lot) or victim characteristics (e.g., a college student). For this reason, it is not generally possible to use this resource for tapping into campus crime. A variety of other methods for monitoring campus crime, exist, however. In particular, the Jeanne Clery Disclosure of Campus Security Policy and Campus Crime Statistics Act (Clery Act) requires colleges and universities that receive federal financial aid to disclose crimes committed on and around campus and provide those data to the U.S. Department of Education (U.S. Department of Education, 2011). Additionally, because many crimes go unreported, surveys have been used to illuminate the "dark figure of crime" on campus. For example, the National Crime Victimization Survey (NCVS), a survey administered to Americans regarding their crime experiences (Bureau of Justice Statistics, 2021) can measure victimization experiences of college students. In the paragraphs below, we review these major classifications of crime measurement.

The Clery Act is federal legislation enacted in 1990 that mandates colleges and universities that participate in federal financial aid programs to maintain crime records and publicize crimes that occur on campus (U.S. Department of Education, 2014). The Snapshot Summary Box 1 below provides further information about the namesake of the law, Jeanne Clery and her legacy.

To this point, much of our discussion has centered on crimes generally. There are, however, special considerations for crimes involving sexual violence. It is a consistent finding that sex offenses are the least reported crimes—both in the general population or on college campuses (Mancini, 2021). For this reason, in 1992, the Clery Act was amended to include the "Campus Sexual Assault Victims' Bill of Rights." This provision requires institutions of higher learning to disclose a summary of university policies related to sexual assault. The policies must address three topics: the rights of sexual assault victims, disciplinary procedures in the university, and educational programs

1.1

Snapshot Summary

Jeanne Clery's Legacy

Like many incoming freshmen, Jeanne Clery started her first semester in college by moving into a dormitory on the campus of Lehigh University in 1985. Sadly for Jeanne, she would not live to see her sophomore year. On April 5, 1986 she was brutally assaulted and murdered in her dorm room. The perpetrator was a fellow student. In the wake of Jeanne's death her parents, Constance and Howard Clery, were horrified to learn that Lehigh University was far from a safe haven. In the three-year period prior to Jeanne's murder, there had been close to 40 violent crimes committed at the small university—6 times more than the number of offenses committed at larger schools in the state (Gross & Fine, 1990). The Clery family was even more shocked to discover that no formal system of crime reporting existed at the time. Over the course of the next four years, Mr. and Mrs. Clery tirelessly advocated for the adoption of more stringent and transparent crime reporting laws nationally. In 1990, their dream was realized with the creation of the Jeanne Clery Disclosure of Campus Security Policy and Campus Crime Statistics Act, or "Clery Act" (U.S. Department of Education, 2014). The federal law requires that institutions of higher learning that participate in federal financial aid programs address two areas related to crime and emergency management:

1. Collect and disseminate information to the public and government about crime or suspicious incidents reported on campus or near the institution. Examples of this task include:
   - maintaining daily crime or incident log information open to public inspection
   - distributing crime security report to university community on a yearly basis
   - submitting crime reports to the U.S. Department of Education annually

2. Incorporate and follow emergency planning policies addressing possible criminal threats or crisis incidents. Specific procedures illustrative of this duty comprise the following:
   - Disclosing emergency planning procedures to the university on a consistent basis
   - Issuing timely warnings to students, faculty, and staff about on-going threats on campus
   - Establishing and publicize missing student notification procedures

Concerned about crime on your campus or prospective college? Check out this U.S. Department of Education website that provides Clery Act reports by year and institution: https://studentaid.gov/data-center/school/clery-act-reports

---

(e.g., awareness of sexual assault to incoming freshmen). In 2014, the Violence Against Women Act (VAWA), a federal law designed to address sexual assault and gender-related crimes, was expanded to include other forms of gender-based violence, such as those crimes that occur in post-secondary institutions (Cantalupo, 2014). Known as the Campus Sexual Violence Elimination Act, or Campus SaVE Act it mandates additional transparency involving reporting procedures, standards for conducting disciplinary review procedures, and increased attention to educational awareness (e.g., bystander programs). These changes have been motivated to increase reporting of sex crimes and better address sexual violence on campus (Marshall, 2014). Because the Clery and SaVE Act mandate other provisions besides reporting, we will discuss them in much greater detail in the next chapter.

In 2020, the federal government in a 13 page addendum (having rescinded

© Tyler Olson/Shutterstock.com

the previous 265 page Handbook on Clery) clarifies that the U.S. Department of Education's Clery Act Compliance Division is authorized to investigate alleged violations and can issue various punishments (U.S. Department of Education, 2020). For example, institutions who violate Clery could face a warning, civil penalties of at least $59,017 per violation of the Act, and the suspension or reduction of federal student aid eligibility (Clery Center, 2021). Clearly, these punitive measures can adversely affect the reputation of an institution and its student body. Thus, colleges and universities have great incentive to comply with the federal requirements.

Reflection 1.1

Clery Act Knowledge

Do you recall hearing about the Clery Act prior to reading this book? Some institutions discuss crime reporting during orientation. Was this your experience? Would learning about the extent of crime on campus have influenced your decision to attend a particular school? Why or why not?

The Clery Act though can only provide information about known offenses. What about those crimes that occur but never come to the attention of the institution or law enforcement? These offenses constitute the "dark figure of crime" (Skogan, 1977), and the simple answer is we may never know about them. However, "unofficial" methods have been developed to tap, at least into a portion, of these unknown crimes. Two types include victimization surveys and self-reports. Below, we discuss each of these types in detail.

Victimization surveys involve asking victims about their crime experiences—whether these offenses were reported or not. When focusing on campus crime, specialized victimization surveys have been developed. Perhaps the most prominent is the National Crime Victimization Survey (NCVS) conducted by the U.S. Census Bureau (Bureau of Justice Statistics, 2021). This survey is administered to the general population on a consistent or longitudinal basis, following a panel sample of Americans age 12 and older for two years and measuring their victimization experiences every six months or so. Special procedures permit the NCVS to compare and contrast victimization among college students versus those in the general population.

Another survey, the Campus Sexual Assault Study (CSA) also measures victimization about college students, but focuses exclusively on sexually related offenses. The survey is distinct from the NCVS as it includes a more expansive definition of sexual assault (Sinozich & Langton, 2014). For example, it is one of the first to generate estimates of the prevalence of drug-facilitated sexual assault (DFSA) among a college sample. It was first administered in 2007 to randomly selected students attending two universities. So far, only one wave of data, 2007, currently exists. Unlike the design of the NCVS, this means it is not possible to track trends in victimization among college students. Additionally, because the CSA only investigates sexual assault among college students, there is no way to compare these experiences with those in the general population.

Universities and other interested organizations and researchers might also conduct their own versions of victimization or climate surveys. One of the most recent and comprehensive of these is a survey entitled the "Campus Climate Survey on Sexual Assault and Sexual Misconduct" that has been deployed twice by the Association of American Universities (AAU; hereafter the CCS). It was first administered to a sample of students attending universities and colleges in 2015 (Cantor et al., 2015), a time when concern about campus sex crime was particularly high. It was deployed again in 2019 (Cantor et al., 2019). It asks students from these diverse institutions about their sexual assault experiences, perceptions of services and how institutions handle sexual assault and harassment complaints, the extent to which they have witnessed sexual assault committed against others, and various demographic information such as class standing and gender identity (Cantor et al., 2015; Cantor et al., 2019).

Another example that includes other crime experiences are studies conducted by researchers, typically professors and faculty working at research universities. Such studies typically seek to answer specific research questions and test hypotheses about crime. In the past criminologists have explored the extent to which college students experience stalking and intimate partner violence (Nobles, Reyns, Fox, & Fisher, 2014), hate crime victimization (DeKeseredy, Nolan, & Hall-Sanchez, 2019), hazing (Allan, Kerschner, & Payne, 2019), cyber-crime (Mikkola et al., 2020), sexual violence (Daigle, Johnston, Azimi, & Felix, 2019), and property crime (Reyns, Sween, & Randa, 2021).

Self-reports are another unofficial way to measure campus crime. Instead of assessing victimization, these surveys ask college students to admit to prior criminal or deviant behavior. For example, some studies have evaluated the amount of cyber-related offending (Morris & Higgins, 2008; Wick, et al., 2017), illicit drug (Arria, Caldeira, Allen, Bugbee, Vincent, & O'Grady, 2017; McCabe, Knight, Teter, & Wechsler, 2005) and alcohol use (Foster, Caravelis, & Kopak, 2014; Wechsler, Lee, Nelson, & Kuo, 2002), and perpetration of sex offenses (Walsh et al., 2020) among college students. Both official and unofficial crime data help paint a portrait of the crime problem on campus. In the paragraphs that follow the prevalence of crime on campus is detailed.

Crime Prevalence and Trends

Now that we have reviewed how crime is measured across our nation's colleges and universities, what do we know about the extent of it? Separately, what do we know about trends in campus crime? As you can now appreciate, measuring crime is no easy endeavor. Having said that, we can turn to national studies that have estimated the prevalence of crime among college students.

In 2005, the NCVS published one of the only reports analyzing violent crime trends among college students and similarly aged people not attending college from 1995–2002 (Baum & Klaus, 2005). This is an important distinction because without a "control group" (i.e., individuals of similar-age not attending college), it would be difficult to understand whether college students are unique in their victimization experiences or if their experiences are simply due to age. Over this seven-year period, college students experienced 60.7 criminal incidents per year. Specifically, this translates into 3.8 rapes/sexual assaults, 5 robberies, 13.5 aggravated assaults, and 38.4 simple assaults annually per 1,000 persons aged 18–24. In comparison, non-college students experienced a higher yearly rate of 75.3 violent crimes. Disaggregating by crime type, these individuals experienced, on average, 4.1 rapes/sexual assaults, 9.5 robberies, 17.7 aggravated assaults, and 44.1 simple assaults per 1,000 people aged 18–24. These statistics (depicted in Snapshot Summary Box 2) show that compared to the general population of similarly-aged Americans college students are less likely to be victims of serious and violent crimes.

A more recent examination conducted by criminologist Bradford Reyns and colleagues (2021) analyzed NCVS data from 2017–2019 that documented the extent of victimization among individuals 18–24, controlling for whether one was enrolled in a college or university (approximately 46 percent of the sample). Overall, less than

Snapshot Summary

1.2 National Crime Victimization Survey Trends from 1995–2002, for Select Crimes

Robbery rates against college students and nonstudents, 1995–2002

Rate of robbery per 1,000, age 18–24

Nonstudents

College students

1996   1998   2000   2002

Aggravated assault rates against college students and nonstudents, 1995–2002

Rate of aggravated assault per 1,000

Nonstudents age 18–24

College students age 18–24

1996   1998   2000   2002

Simple assault rates against college students and nonstudents, 1995–2002

Rate of simple assault per 1,000, age 18–24

Nonstudents

College students

1996   1998   2000   2002

Source: Bureau of Justice Statistics; Retrieved from: http://www.bjs.gov/index.cfm?ty=pbdetail&iid=593

1 percent and 3 percent of the total sample experienced either violent and property crime, respectively. In line with prior NCVS results, the study showed that simply being a student had no influence on the likelihood of experiencing victimization. However, supporting the argument that college students may have unique crime risks, students who lived on campus had increased risk of violent and property victimization compared to students who did not live on campus.

Other research (Wang, Chen, Zhang, & Oudekerk, 2020), though excluding a "control" group of individuals not attending college, has explored more recent prevalence rates of campus crime. Overall, the researchers estimated a crime rate of 19.6 per 10,000 full-time students in 2017 (the most recent year under study). According to an analysis of multiple official data sources (i.e., known and/or reported offenses), this equates to 28,900 offenses committed on postsecondary institutions annually which were reported to police or other security officials. Most offenses involved burglaries (11,100) and sex crimes (10,400).

Given the special emphasis on addressing college sex crime, in 2014, the NCVS released findings from a special study examining the prevalence of sexual assault among women (Sinozich & Langton, 2014). The study is distinct from the earlier report (Baum & Klaus, 2005) as it limits analysis to sexual victimization, and also extends the reference period. In the study frame (1995–2013), women ages 18–24 had the highest rate of sexual victimizations compared to women in other age groups. Over this time, non-students reported significantly more sexual assaults (7.6 sexual victimizations per 1,000 women) than students (6.1 sexual victimizations per 1,000 women). Sinozich and Langton (2014) also analyzed the type of sexual victimization. In particular, 33 percent of students reported a "completed rape" ("unlawful penetration of a person"), compared to 40 percent of non-students. By comparison, 25 percent of college women were the victims of "attempted rape" ("an attempt to commit unlawful penetration of a person"), compared to 24 percent of non-students.

A slightly higher percentage of college students, 31 percent, experienced "sexual assault" ("unwanted sexual contact" short of unlawful penetration such as fondling); 28 percent of non-students were victims of these offenses. A much smaller proportion of both college and non-student females reported threats of sexual violence (11 percent versus 8 percent, respectively).

One other earlier victimization study commissioned by the federal government relied on responses from a random sample of over 4,000 women attending a college or university in the fall of 1996 (Fisher, Cullen, & Turner, 2000). Thus, in contrast to the NCVS study, it is cross-sectional in nature—asking only about victimization during a specific time period rather than over the course of time. Still, the survey method was notable because it utilized behaviorally specific questions regarding sexual victimization (i.e., instead of simply asking "have you been raped during your college career"). Fisher and colleagues (2000, p. 5) instruct that this is an advancement over prior research because "a respondent may not answer 'yes' to a screen question unless it is worded in a way that reflects the experience the respondent has had." Analysis of the survey data revealed that 2.8 percent of the sample had experienced either a completed rape (1.7 percent) or an attempted rape incident (1.1 percent). The victimization rate was 27.7 rapes per 1,000 female students.

Recall too that the AAU, a non-profit organization dedicated to advancing postsecondary interests, commissioned two waves of its campus climate survey (CCS). While not a federally-sponsored survey, study findings are relevant toward understanding the nature and extent of campus sexual assault. In the first wave of administration (2015) 13 percent of students reported experiencing a "nonconsensual sexual contact by physical force or inability to consent since entering school." In particular, certain groups—women and "transgender, genderqueer, questioning or not listed" (TGQN) students—reported a higher prevalence rate of contact than male and graduate/professional students. In the later wave (2019), a greater extent of assaults were reported. Specifically, the extent of assaults increased by 3 percent for female undergraduates, 2.4 percent for graduate and professional women, and 1.4 percent for undergraduate men (Cantor et al., 2015; Cantor et al., 2019).

Across all of these data sources it is clear that compared to their non-student counterparts, college students are significantly less likely to report their victimization to police. Baum and Klaus (2005) revealed that close to 50 percent of nonstudents reported their offenses to law enforcement, whereas only 35 percent of college students did so. The later government-sponsored survey, conducted by Sinozich and Langton (2014), found that while approximately 1 in 3 Americans report their sexual victimization to police, only 1 in 5 college students do so. Although the AAU CCS study, the most recent investigation into college sexual assault, did not include a comparable "control" group, it did gauge reporting patterns among students (Cantor et al., 2015; Cantor et al., 2019). It confirms this pattern of underreporting. Specifically, in 2015, 25 percent of students who described experiencing a serious penetrative offense reported the crime to police, and similarly low reporting rates were captured in the 2019 wave.

This leads us to the question of why people would choose not to report a crime committed against them. Fortunately, the NCVS and AAU posed this very question to respondents. For both nonstudents and students, the top three reasons given for not reporting in the NCVS were as follows: "private or personal matter" (30.7 percent of students versus 26.8 percent of nonstudents), "minor crime/no loss" (24.7 percent of students versus 19.1 percent of nonstudents), and "reported to another official" (8.5 percent of students versus 9.3 percent of nonstudents). Students cited similar concerns in the AAU. In that survey, the reasons for non-reporting among students related to emotional distress, the concern that the offense was not serious enough, and lack of confidence about accountability (Cantor et al., 2015; Cantor et al., 2019).

Beyond measuring sexual assault, other work has explored the extent to which college students experience bias or hate crime victimization. In a recent examination of over 5,000 students attending a larger unnamed university, approximately 60 percent indicated that they were victims of a hate crime, or an offense motivated by one's "real or perceived race/ethnicity, national origin, religion, sex, sexual orientation, physical or mental disability, or political orientation" (DeKeseredy et al., 2019, p. 1). Most students indicated that they experienced verbal abuse and harassment but a non-trivial percentage, nearly 20 percent, also reported being *physically* victimized or "sexually touched" without their consent (p. 8).

Additionally, students may be at increased risk of experiencing unique types of crime due to their lifestyle. For this reason, recent scholarship has explored hazing experiences among the college population. Generally, hazing refers to "any activity expected of someone joining or participating in a group (such as a student club, organization, or team) that humiliates, degrades, abuses, or endangers regardless of a person's willingness to participate" (Hoover & Pollard, 1999, p. 8). In a national analysis of close to 6,000 students attending seven universities, a little over one-quarter of students active in social organizations (e.g., clubs, sports) experienced hazing, and close to 70 percent claimed to be aware of hazing incidents on campus (Allan et al., 2019). The most frequent types of hazing victimizations involved high-risk drinking ("drinking games"), social isolation, and "personal servitude."

Reflection 1.2

Reporting Prevalence

Why might college students be less likely to report sexual assault compared to similarly-aged peers in the general population? How might universities and colleges address these obstacles to reporting?

Recall that in addition to victimization surveys, self-reports, or surveys that inquire about criminal or deviant behavior (as opposed to victimization) can also help us illuminate the "dark figure" of unreported crime. Indeed, researchers have concentrated their efforts on investigating crimes that appear widespread across universities—cyber-related offenses, drug and alcohol crimes, and sexual victimization. In their seminal study, Morris and Higgins (2008) asked students attending two unidentified universities whether they have ever engaged in digital piracy (e.g., downloading illegal copies of music or videos). Over 60 percent of the sample reported at least one type of piracy, and nearly 40 percent participated in multiple acts of piracy.

Other studies have investigated alcohol and drug use among college students. A little more than 30 percent of college students report binge drinking in the last year (Schulenberg, Johnston, O'Malley, Bachman, Miech, & Patrick, 2020). The use of illicit drugs, with the exception of marijuana use, appears less widespread than underage drinking, but still problematic. Monitoring the Future (MTF) data (a national self-report survey funded by the federal government) show that "other" illicit drug use (i.e., excluding marijuana use) in the last year was less prevalent than binge drinking, with 5.6 percent of college students reporting cocaine use, 3.7 percent reporting hallucinogen ("LSD") use, and 3.3 percent reporting ecstasy or "Molly" use (Schulenberg et al., 2020). However, 43 percent of college students report using marijuana at least once in the prior year (Schulenberg et al., 2020).

It has also been acknowledged that prescription drug abuse is prevalent among the general population, and this may extend to young people. For this reason, the MTF survey measures the extent of prescription drug misuse among college students. The most recent waves found that less than 3 percent of college students report abusing opioids and 8 percent report misusing amphetamines such as Adderall (Schulenberg et al., 2020).

What about more serious, interpersonal crimes? Given concerns about sexual victimization on campus, researchers have turned to self-report data to assess the prevalence of sexual assault. In a 2021 meta-analysis (i.e., a review of all research in a particular area), Anderson and colleagues synthesized results across 78 independent samples of men attending college who completed a self-report concerning their previous sexual assault perpetration. They found that on average, 29 percent of the men described engaging in behaviors consistent with sex offending. The authors observe that there was wide methodological and variation across studies (e.g., sample size, type of questions on the self-report), meaning this estimate should be interpreted with caution. For example, "verbal coercion" (operationalized as "any type of sexual intercourse obtained via verbal tactics such as verbal pressuring behavior, expressions of anger, threats to the relationship, and so on") was more common, suggesting that 19 percent of college men have engaged in such behaviors (Anderson et al., 2021, p. 485). The percentage of college men who have engaged in behaviors fitting the legal definition of "rape" (defined as "any type of sexual intercourse obtained via incapacitation, physical force, or threats of physical force") was 6.5 percent. Regardless of methodological variation, the results of this large scale and most recent review indicate that sexual assault perpetration is problematic on the average college campus.

To recap prevalence findings, college students experience less violent victimization than their non-college counterparts. Even so, reporting of crime is low and this undoubtedly suggests that we underestimate crime prevalence among this special population. Furthermore, self-report studies suggest that many crimes, the less serious (such as digital piracy and drug use) and more serious, interpersonal and violent crimes (e.g., sexual assaults) are committed against those attending universities and colleges nationwide. These data though, tell us only part of the crime story. That is, what have been trends in crime among college students?

To understand trends in crime it is essential that we analyze longitudinal data—that is data collected across various points in time. This is in contrast to "cross-sectional" data, or "snapshot" data, collected at one point in time. Here again, we can rely on NCVS data since it is consistently collected by the U.S. Census Bureau. According to the most recent NCVS trend data released by the federal government, crime involving college students has substantially declined (Baum & Klaus, 2005). In particular, between 1995 and 2002 rates of violent crime decreased by 54 percent. Non-students also experienced a reduction in victimization risk, but to a lesser extent—for them, the violent crime rate declined by 45 percent over this seven-year period. The most dramatic drop for both groups involved the following crime classifications: robbery offenses (66 percent and 44 percent decline for students and non-students, respectively) simple assault (58 percent and 49 percent decline for students and non-students, respectively), and aggravated assault (37 percent and 41 percent decline for students and non-students, respectively).

Other longitudinal data examining reported offenses involving college students indicates a historic (i.e., long-term) decline like the Baum and Klaus (2005) investigation, but more recently, a trend in the upward direction. Similar to the earlier investigation, Wang et al. (2020) in analyzing Clery (reported) data find an overall decline in campus crime from 2001 to 2017, specifically, the overall prevalence of campus crimes reported to police or university officials declined by 31 percent over this period. However, in disaggregating this overall trend, from 2014 to 2017, the reported crime rate increased by 8 percent. Notably however, this drive may be attributable to the substantial increase in reported sex crimes. In particular, the Wang et al. (2020) analysis indicates a significant jump in reported sex crime, nearly 16 percent from 2016 to 2017. While this analysis does not permit us to compare the victimization experiences of similarly-aged non-college students like in the earlier Baum and Klaus (2005) report, it is helpful for understanding more contemporary trends. A depiction can be found in Summary Snapshot Box 3.

Given that Clery (i.e., reported) data indicate a surge in violent crime, driven primarily by an increase in reported sexual assaults, we now turn to a special discussion of sexual victimization. According to the 2014 NCVS survey which tracked sexual assault among students and those of college-age not attending a university (Sinozich & Langton, 2014), the rate for sexual assault among both groups has substantially declined since 1997. In that year, the sexual victimization rate among college students was 9.2 and for non-students, 7.9. In 2013, those estimates decreased for both

Snapshot Summary

1.3 Criminal Incidents at Postsecondary Institutions, 2001–2017

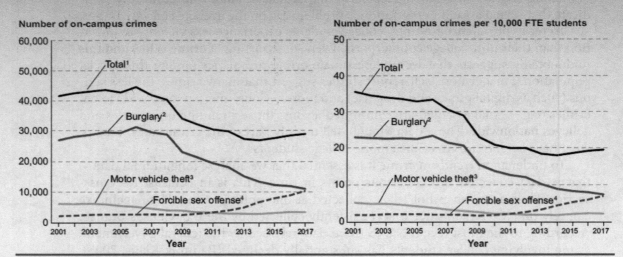

[1] Includes other reported crimes not separately shown.
[2] Unlawful entry of a structure to commit a felony or theft.
[3] Theft or attempted theft of a motor vehicle.
[4] Any sexual act directed against another person forcibly and/or against that person's will.
NOTE: Data are for degree-granting institutions, which are institutions that grant associate's or higher degrees and participate in Title IV federal financial aid programs. Some institutions that report Clery Act data—specifically, non-degree-granting institutions and institutions outside of the 50 states and the District of Columbia—are excluded from this figure. Crimes include incidents involving students, staff, and on-campus guests. Excludes off-campus crimes even if they involve college students or staff. Some data have been revised from previously published figures.
SOURCE: U.S. Department of Education, Office of Postsecondary Education, Campus Safety and Security Reporting System, 2001 through 2017; and National Center for Education Statistics, Integrated Postsecondary Education Data System (IPEDS), Spring 2002 through Spring 2018, Fall Enrollment component.

Source: National Center for Education Statistics (NCES) https://nces.ed.gov/pubs2020/2020063.pdf

groups—the sexual victimization rate for students was 4.4 and for non-students, 4.3. Other victimization studies sought to identify trends in sexual victimization across a college career. For example, Krebs and colleagues (2007) using an online survey administered to college students at two universities (N = 6,800) in the winter of 2006 estimated that if such statistics were extrapolated, nearly one in five women will experience an attempted or completed sexual assault over the typical course of their collegiate education.

In understanding sexual victimization trends among students, we can also turn to the AAU CCS, since there has been more than one wave of data collection. There are of course caveats here regarding generalizability, or more simply, the ability to compare. For example, there were some changes in the survey instrument (that is, the survey questions posed to college students) in 2019 (Cantor et al., 2019). Additionally, the second wave of the AAU included student samples from other universities than in the first (2015) wave. In all, this means results are not exactly comparable. Still, there was a small increase in the percentage of students, approximately 13 percent, who reported experiencing nonconsensual sexual contact ("by physical force or inability to consent") in 2019 (up nearly 2 percent from the 2015 estimate).

The combined use of "official" and "unofficial" data allow us to "triangulate," or turn to official statistics to compare and contrast trends across the different modes of analysis. Triangulation assumes that if multiple data sources reveal a similar pattern we can have greater confidence in that collective interpretation. While crimes involving students may be on the decline from a long-term historic perspective (2001 to 2017), across both official and unofficial data sources, there is some indication of an increase in sex offenses. It is difficult to identify the precise factors driving this increase. With this caveat in mind, it may be in part due to the popularity of the 2017 #MeToo, a social movement, which emphasized holding perpetrators of sexual assault accountable for their crimes (Mancini, 2021). Accordingly, #MeToo may have increased personal acknowledgement of sexual victimization (driving up "unofficial" data) and at the same time, increased the likelihood for individuals to officially report to law enforcement. Of course, future studies will need to evaluate whether this trend holds over longer periods. For now, it is noteworthy to mention that the recent increase in campus crime is driven largely by crimes of a sexual nature.

Crime Patterns

In addition to studying the *amount* of crime, criminologists have also worked to uncover factors associated with victimization on campus. We generally call these relationships "crime patterns." Once again the NCVS data are particularly instructive for understanding these relationships nationally given that the survey asks college students specific details about the victim, the offense, and perpetrator. In the 2005 survey (Baum & Klaus), males and Whites, compared to females, and students of other races, were significantly more likely to experience violent crime.

Beyond these demographic differences, what is known about offense characteristics? The Baum and Klaus (2005) survey is again helpful for addressing this question. According to this federal report, most violent crimes (excluding sexual offenses) against college students were committed by stranger offenders (58 percent). Specific patterns are evident concerning time and place. An overwhelming majority (93 percent) of crimes against students occurred off campus and in the evening (72 percent; 6 pm to 6 am). One in four offenses were committed in an "open area" or "the street," 18 percent in a "commercial place" (e.g., a bar, mall), 17 percent in a private residence (excluding the victim's), 11 percent in the victim's residence, and 9 percent in a parking garage or lot. Turning to other characteristics, most students reported not experiencing a physical injury in relation to their victimization (75 percent). However, of those who were physically hurt, most (59 percent) did not receive medical treatment.

The NCVS also solicits information about perceived characteristics of perpetrators. Here, 41 percent of students reported that they believed the person who assaulted them was under the influence of alcohol or drugs. A much smaller amount (6 percent) of victims judged the perpetrator of the crime to be part of a gang. Most violent offenses did not involve a weapon, such as a knife or a gun (66 percent).

Recall that our discussion has largely focused on violent victimization as a broad category. The circumstances involving sexual victimization follow distinct patterns, however. Sinozich and Langton (2014) for instance recount that although most violent crimes involve a stranger perpetrator, in rape and sexual assault cases, nearly 80 percent of students knew the offender.

There are other differences in patterns across violent crime and sexual victimization. Most of the latter category involved a female victim (83 percent). The 2014 report revealed few race and ethnicity differences in risk of sexual victimization. Among female college students, the rate of victimization was similar for Whites and African American students (6.7 vs. 6.1 per 1,000, respectively). However, compared to these groups, Hispanics had a significantly lower rate of rape and sexual assault (4.5 per 1,000). College women in the 18–19 age category had the highest rate of sexual victimization (6.6 per 1,000 women), followed by females aged 22–24 (6 per 1,000 women); students in the 20–21 age category reported the lowest rate of sexual victimization (5.8 per 1,000 females). Regional characteristics (not assessed in the earlier study by Baum & Klaus, 2005) in sexual victimization risk were also assessed. To illustrate, female students in the Midwest had the highest risk of being raped or sexually assaulted, followed by students living in the Northeast; students in the South reported the lowest rates of sexual victimization (Sinozich & Langton, 2014).

Most student victims (51 percent) were sexually assaulted or raped away from home pursuing leisure activities or traveling from one location to another. Almost two-thirds of students were sexually victimized in the evening (6 pm to 6 am). In contrast to findings from violent victimization patterns, a majority of sex crime victims reported experiencing a physical injury (57 percent); most students (60 percent) received no treatment for these injuries. Furthermore, a large majority of victims (82 percent) reported that the perpetrator did not use a weapon during the offense. Unlike the earlier violent victimization study, this recent wave of victimization data provides additional details regarding offender characteristics. In their study, Sinozich and Langton (2014) relayed that most victims were assaulted by one offender (95 percent), perceived the perpetrator to be White (63 percent), male (97 percent), and younger, around the 18–29 age range (68 percent). Alcohol or drug use by the offender was suspected in nearly half (47 percent) of sex crime assaults against students.

What has other research uncovered regarding patterns of crime among college students? Put differently, what appear to be other risk factors for victimization while attending an institution of higher learning? Some smaller-scale studies have found specific characteristics of the location of the institution to increase victimization. For instance, higher unemployment in a general community has been associated with greater campus victimization (McPheters, 1978). At least one study has linked campus crime, specifically, robberies and motor vehicle thefts with the presence of nearby casinos (Hyclak, 2011). Other studies have uncovered criminogenic effects of the college itself. Institutional-level factors, such as costs of room and board, number of full-time students, and number of students residing in dormitories have been linked to higher crime rates among students (Bromley, 1995; Fernandez & Lizotte, 1995).

Separately, other work has explored how victim characteristics might influence crime rates. College students have lifestyles that appear to differ from the general public. That is, they may be more likely to have leisure time and attend social events;

they may also experiment with illicit drugs, or engage in other activities that influence victimization risk. It follows that these behaviors and traits could influence victimization. Some research supports this assertion. In a seminal study of 12 colleges, Fisher, Sloan, Cullen, and Lu (1998) discovered that few demographic variables (e.g., race, sex) contributed to violent victimization; rather lifestyle factors such as attending parties on campus and engaging in recreational drug use, were significantly predictive of experiencing a violent offense. In contrast, increased property victimization was associated with younger age, being African American, being a member of an athletic team, residing in an all-male or co-ed dorm, spending more nights on campus, being a full-time student, and the overall theft rate of the university.

A later study, which analyzed the risk of experiencing crime among college students and similar aged peers found that being a college student actually protected individuals from crime (Reyns et al., 2021). Specifically, college students were significantly less likely compared to people not attending a post-secondary institution to experience violent (excluding sexual assault) and property crime. However, no protective effect for students emerged in preventing sexual assault. Among students, those living on campus were at significantly greater risk of experiencing both violent and property victimization. Location of residence had no effect on the likelihood of experiencing sexual assault. In predicting the risk of sexual assault for female students, the only distinction in the Reyns et al. (2021) study was that lower income college women faced the highest risk. Non-heterosexual students were more likely to be victims of sexual assault than heterosexual students across gender. Finally, having experienced a prior victimization was a significant predictor of sexual assault, regardless of gender. The Reyns et al. (2021) investigation is notable for revealing new findings concerning risk levels of campus victimization and also replicates many findings from previous research.

As previously reviewed in our discussion of victimization prevalence, DeKeseredy and colleagues (2020) studied the nature and extent of hate crime victimization. While a majority of the 5,000 students under that investigation indicated experiencing a hate crime in the past, there was variation in student risk levels. For example, LGBTQ students were nearly twice as likely as non-LGBTQ students to report experiencing a bias offense. Other students were also at increased risk, such as students who were involved with political and/or social action groups, Latino/Hispanic students, and students who lived off campus.

Research examining hazing victimization also indicates divides across risk levels. Specifically, this work has found that male students and students more enmeshed in university life—those for example, participating in a sports organization/team, or "Greek Life" (sorority/fraternity membership)—tend to face a greater risk of experiencing hazing than female students and those not involved in such organizations (Allan et al., 2019).

What about factors that may be *negatively* related to victimization risk? These are called "protective factors" and a number have been identified by prior research. In the influential Fisher et al. (1998) study, several were correlated with a reduction in violent crime and property offenses. Attending a non-mandatory crime prevention awareness program reduced violent victimization likelihood. By comparison, higher academic standing, being a member of a fraternity or sorority, asking someone to watch property while left unattended, and the percent of students who live on campus were associated with reduced theft victimization.

Given concern about sexual violence on campus, some scholarship has specifically investigated protective factors related to sexual victimization. Here, three factors have been uncovered. "Sexual conservatism" (e.g., fewer sexual encounters) reduced the incidence of sexual victimization of college students in at least two studies (Himelein, 1995; Koss & Dinero, 1980). In contrast, other research has demonstrated that "assertiveness" with the opposite sex (measured using a scale with items such as, "saying no," "setting limits," "arguing") and religiosity (i.e., regular atten-dance at religious services) reduces the probability of experiencing sexual victim-ization (MacGreene & Navarro, 1998; Mynatt & Allgrier, 1990; generally, Hirsch & Khan, 2020). To be sure, prior research has disproportionately examined risk as op-posed to protective factors. Because the latter may be critical in developing crime prevention programs on campus, future research will need to work toward illumi-nating additional factors. Given the importance of ensuring campus safety, we will revisit crime prevention research in the third section of the book. Before moving on to the next unit summarizing responses to campus crime, be sure to test your recall about crime measurement by completing the Chapter 1 Exercise.

Crime Measurement

As described earlier, estimating the amount of crime that occurs annually in the U.S. is fraught with difficulties. Using what you have learned in this chapter, first think about the strengths and negatives of the following crime measurement systems: official data, victimization data, and self-report data. Then answer the questions measuring your mastery of these important chapter concepts. The web links below provide further context for understanding these data sources:

http://www.fbi.gov/about-us/cjis/ucr/ucr
http://www.bjs.gov/index.cfm?ty=dcdetail&iid=245
https://www.ncjrs.gov/criminal_justice2000/vol_4/04c.pdf

1. Official Record Data

   Description? _____

   Strengths? _____

   Limitations? _____

2. Victimization Survey Data

   Description? _____

   Strengths? _____

   Limitations? _____

3. Self-Report Survey Data

   Description? _____

   Strengths? _____

   Limitations? _____

4. What is the "dark figure of crime" and how does it apply toward understanding the extent of crime in the U.S.?

5. If someone close to you was concerned about victimization and asked you to describe whether crime on campus has decreased, increased, or remained the same, what would you say? Be sure to mention the evidence you are drawing on to support your response.

6. What is known about reporting patterns of college students compared to individuals in the general population? What factors might explain these patterns?

Addressing Campus Crime 2

1. How have institutions responded to crime threats on campus?

2. What is the prevalence of campus police agencies nationally and what are the duties of campus law enforcement?

3. How do disciplinary review boards work and what are their shortcomings?

4. What pieces of legislation exist to combat campus crime?

5. What new policies and procedures are currently being considered or implemented by the nation's colleges and universities?

6. What have institutions done to educate students about crime?

7. How have universities addressed the needs of victims?

LEARNING GOALS

- To understand how institutions have responded to and addressed crimes against students.
- To demonstrate knowledge of the strengths and limitations of these responses.
- To acknowledge new procedures to curtail campus crime.

High profile crimes on campus such as mass shootings and sexual assault cases have captivated national attention. In turn, institutions of higher learning and the federal government have responded in kind, incorporating a range of measures designed to respond to campus threats. Chapter 2 reviews six major efforts: campus law enforcement, disciplinary review boards, current federal laws, new legislative initiatives, education, and victim services. As a student, you are a direct consumer of these responses. For this reason, comprehending the diversity of ways your respective institution has responded to the crime problem has practical utility for your personal safety and that of your colleagues and friends.

Campus Law Enforcement

Up until this point, we have analyzed the nature and extent of campus crime and victimization. We now concentrate on reviewing how crime is addressed on the typical college campus. A natural starting point is to first examine the use of campus policing. The first emergence of the use of campus law enforcement is traced to the aftermath of the Kent State massacre, an incident that involved the shooting death of several protesting students by the Ohio National Guard in 1970. Following this horrific event, university administrators began to call for legislative support for the creation of campus police agencies (Nelson, 2015).

The use of police departments to respond to campus crime problems has only continued since then. According to the most recent federal statistics (Reaves, 2015), 77 percent of post-secondary institutions with at least 2,500 attending students reported using sworn officers. This percentage has risen by two percent from the 2004–2005 school year (the first time the federal government surveyed campus law enforcement personnel). In the 2011–2012 school year universities and colleges with sworn personnel employed 24 full time officers; per 1,000 students, this translates into 2.4 officers. This represents a 10 percent increase in officers from the 2004–2005 survey. Overall, this federal data indicate that colleges and universities have increased their police presence. Snapshot Summary Box 4 describes what it is like to be a campus law enforcement officer.

© John Roman Images/Shutterstock.com

Beyond the extent of policing on campus, though, what is known about other aspects—such as jurisdictional boundaries and specific policing activities? According to the 2015 report (Reaves, 2015), most law enforcement personnel had the authority to arrest individuals on property adjacent to campus (86 percent) and properties outside the area surrounding campus (71 percent). Significantly fewer campus law enforcement officers had arrest powers statewide (35 percent). Thus, most policing activity is limited to the campus and surrounding areas.

In addition to apprehending suspects and investigating crime, police agencies nationally have also been involved in educational and crime prevention efforts on campus. At least three-quarters of law enforcement agencies in the 2011–2012 academic year participated in general crime prevention, rape prevention, drug and alcohol education, self-defense training, and stalking prevention (Reaves, 2015). A smaller number of agencies (less than 60 percent) created and delivered other programs—such as awareness and prevention of cyber-crime, bias/hate offenses, and white-collar crime. Moreover, most police departments (88 percent) nationally provided safety escort services for students, faculty, and staff. This service is designed to reduce crime and fear of it by accompanying concerned community members to areas on and around campus.

Snapshot Summary

4

Campus Law Enforcement as a Career

Qualifications	Salary	Responsibilities
• High school diploma; college degree or experience may also be required • Basic training—can last for 6 months (the "academy") • On-going educational, legal, and physical agility training	• $27,500 median annual salary for officers • Salary may be supplemented with signing bonuses, extra personal days, tuition stipends • Leadership position salaries range from $40,000 to $100,000	• Patrol campus and surrounding areas • Enforce all federal, state, and municipal/county laws and regulations in investigation and arrest procedures and adhere to relevant university policies • Follow Clery Act Reporting requirements • Educate university community about crime risk and prevention • Provide support and services to students, faculty, staff, and larger community • Work with referring agencies (e.g., city police)

Source: Information detailed in Snapshot Summary Box 3 was retrieved from http://www.lawenforcementedu.net/police-officer/campus-police/ and http://www.iaclea.org/visitors/career/index.cfm

© BlueRingMedia/Shutterstock.com

Reflection 3

Campus Police

Does your university have its own police force? If so, where on campus is the department located? Do you ever see or interact with officers? Would you feel comfortable reporting a crime to campus police? Why or why not?

Disciplinary Review Boards

Beyond policing, universities and colleges have unique mechanisms in place for investigating and punishing individuals accused of engaging in criminal behavior against other students or faculty through the use of grievance or disciplinary review boards. Accordingly, these procedures, at least indirectly, address criminal activity on campus. For instance, a university can investigate and ultimately expel students accused of certain behaviors, such as sexual assault. The process is not the same as adjudicating criminal guilt but rather is designed to punish students for violating the student conduct code (Anderson, 2014).

Nationally, in one of the only federal reports to study the issue, over 70 percent of universities report using some type of disciplinary or student conduct board; however, these practices are less common in non-residential colleges, for-profit universities, and 2 year universities (Karjane, Fisher, & Cullen, 2002). Across most schools (80 percent), the standard of guilt is the "preponderance of evidence" standard, a burden applied in civil court. Only 3 percent of schools incorporate the more stringent "beyond a reasonable doubt" standard guaranteed in criminal court. The remaining proportion applies a different standard (Karjane et al., 2002). Notably, in 2011, the federal government under the Obama administration required that institutions use the "preponderance of evidence" standard in adjudicating instances of alleged sexual assault and harassment. However, in 2020, Trump-era revisions took effect, one of which gave schools the discretion to use higher burdens of proof (e.g., "clear and convincing" standards). As of this writing, those provisions stand (U.S. Department of Education, 2020).

According to the Karjane et al. (2002) report, regardless of the standard of proof used, the composition of the boards can vary across institutions, from as few as a single board member to a high of 24. Most universities (51 percent) authorize a 3 to 5 member board to decide the disposition of the cases. A majority of the colleges surveyed disclosed that the boards are typically composed of students (80 percent) and faculty (76 percent); twenty percent include a judicial officer or administrator.

What are the typical sanctions for violations? Karjane and colleagues (2002) note that a range of penalties exist for those found to have violated the student conduct code: loss of privileges, required restitution, censure (official or written reprimand), suspension or probation, and the most serious, expulsion. These punishments of course vary by institution and also by the nature of the violation (Mancini, 2020; Tenerowicz, 2000).

Such disciplinary procedures are not without their criticism. On the one hand, some have questioned whether institutions of higher learning should be tasked with punishing incidents that may also be criminal (Coray, 2016). Universities, for instance, do not typically employ trained detectives or criminal investigators like those used in the justice system. Colleges are also not held to Constitutional standards or case law in collecting and analyzing evidence. The adjudicating body of review boards—typically composed of students, faculty and staff—is also distinct from that used in the criminal courts (i.e., judges and juries). Furthermore, the maximum punishment that can be handed down by a university—expulsion—is clearly not on par with criminal justice system sanctions, such as a prison sentence. Two specific investigations that delved into the issue of punishment are discussed below.

One investigation examining over 100 universities and colleges conducted by the *Columbus Times Dispatch* and the Student Press Law Center (Binkley, Wagner, Riepenhoff, & Gregory, 2014) claims that even under this sanctioning system, universities impose weak sanctions on violators for serious criminal behavior. The report describes a case involving a student found responsible for committing sexual assault receiving a rather limited penalty. He was given a written reprimand, required to leave his campus dorm for a month, and not have any minors as guests. Another striking punishment mentioned in the report involved a University of Toledo student found responsible for his participation in the stabbing death of his roommate. He was not expelled from the school nor ever charged in a criminal court. In short, if these findings are indicative of recent national trends, there is the concern that violators typically do not face the most severe sanction (i.e., expulsion) that can be handed down by post-secondary institutions even for serious offenses involving violence.

One other analysis conducted by the *Washington Post* (Anderson, 2014) examined 2012–2013 survey data from colleges and universities that receive grants from the Justice Department's Office on Violence Against Women regarding internal discipline of sexual misconduct (notably, these data were not previously released by the government but were obtained through a Freedom of Information Act request). The investigation found that of the 478 sanctions handed down for sexual assault, 12 percent were expulsions and 28 percent were suspensions; the remaining 60 percent comprised other sanctions such as counseling or reprimands. Thus, as these two investigations reveal most students accused of serious interpersonal violence are permitted to stay enrolled at their respective institutions.

On the other hand, some have questioned whether due process, particularly for the accused, is upheld during these hearings (Harper, Maskaly, Kirkner, & Lorenz, 2017). Accused students are not afforded the same Constitutional rights that they would be in a criminal proceeding. For instance, in contrast to criminal trial proceedings, conduct board hearings are typically closed to the public and vary across colleges (Binkley et al., 2014). Separately, as mentioned earlier (Karjane et al., 2002), the standard of proof applied to review board hearings is typically much lower (e.g., "preponderance of evidence") than that required in the justice system (i.e., "proof beyond a reasonable doubt").

Perhaps the most concerning aspect of the practice voiced by critics is that universities do not typically publicize their investigations of alleged misconduct or disclose the outcome of proceedings. Institutions of higher learning are bound by the Family and Educational Right to Privacy Act (FERPA, 1991). Although FERPA was designed to protect student privacy by keeping "educational records," such as grades confidential, most schools have extended this protection to disciplinary procedures, including the names of the alleged violator and the outcome of such hearings. Accordingly, the general public and student body are not notified of on-going investigations into what may amount to criminal behavior (e.g., sexual assault) in some cases.

Additionally, universities are not typically required to report when students have been found responsible for having committed a violation and the extent of their punishment. Three exceptions, are notable, though. The Department of Education (2011) requires that schools disclose the number of conduct board hearings for weapon-related violations, drug abuse, and liquor law violations. Still this policy indicates that institutions would not be *required* to report violations regarding serious interpersonal offenses. For this reason, some question whether these procedures contribute to the "dark figure of crime." In response, policymakers have proposed incorporating changes regarding disclosure of disciplinary review proceedings. As briefly mentioned earlier, the Campus SaVE Act mandates greater transparency in conduct board procedures that involve alleged criminal offenses. This legislation and other laws are discussed in greater detail in the next section.

Prominent Legislation

Clery Act. After the tragic murder of Jeanne Clery Jeanne's parents and the parents of other college crime victims advocated for policies that would better protect students. Perhaps partly due to such efforts, in 1990 Congress enacted one of the first pieces of federal legislation to address campus crime—the "Clery Act." Recall that prior to their efforts, colleges and universities were not required to disclose the extent of crime on campus. From a crime prevention standpoint, this practice meant students were not aware of potential dangers or the techniques that might protect them from crime. In particular, the law covers several sections of responsibilities.

First, as briefly mentioned earlier institutions—that is, any college or university that participates in the federal financial aid program—are required to fulfill their *reporting requirements*. In particular, colleges must disclose crime statistics for offenses that occur on campus and in surrounding areas near the college; this includes sorority and fraternity housing and off-campus classrooms. The Clery Act mandates that these statistics cover seven classifications of crime: homicide, sex offenses, robbery, aggravated assault, burglary, motor vehicle theft, and arson. As touched upon earlier, schools must also report arrests and disciplinary procedure action for three other categories: liquor law violations, drug violations, and illegal weapon possession violations. With changes to the Clery Act, institutions must also report suspected hate crimes (or offenses committed because of a victim's perceived race, gender, religion, sexual orientation, ethnicity and disability).

Related to reporting, schools must publicize this information in the form of an official document, the "Annual Security Report," by October 1. It must include three years of prior campus crime data and the institution's crime and victimization policies (e.g., rights guaranteed to victims of sex crime). Federal law mandates that the university community be notified of its publication and given access to it in electronic or hard copy form. The Act also mandates that universities with student housing produce an annual fire safety report. The publication should note reported fires that occur in on-campus housing and maintain a log open to public inspection detailing fire reports.

A final responsibility that relates to reporting involves maintenance of a daily police log. Universities that have a police department must document reported crime information, such as a description of possible criminal incidents, calls for service, or arrests. This information must be publicized and provided to members of the public. An example of this log is shown in Snapshot Summary Box 5.

Beyond reporting requirements, schools are also tasked with implementing *timely emergency response policies, such as notifications and warnings* regarding crime threats and other incidents. This change was motivated in part by the 2007 Virginia Tech mass shootings in which 32 people were killed and 17 seriously injured by a fellow student (Urbina, 2009). There was concern following the massacre that notifications were not given in a timely fashion, exposing students, faculty, and staff to

---

Snapshot Summary

5   **Daily Incident Log at Happy Place University, HPU**

Date of Log (Report #)	Incident Date (Time)	Incident Type	Location	Description	Disposition
2/21/22 (0013569)	2/17/22 (10:05 am)	Theft	The Quad	Student reported cell phone stolen	Pending investigation
2/22/22 (0013570)	2/18/22 (11:45 pm)	Aggravated assault	Happy Place Bar	Staff member advised being hit by two students who attend HPU	Referred to outside agency; pending investigation
2/22/22 (0013571)	2/19/22 (5:06 pm)	Hit and run	Parking Garage	Two students advised that an unknown vehicle struck both of their vehicles and fled the scene	Pending investigation

unnecessary danger. Given this concern, the alerts—in the form of e-mails, text messages, or phone calls—are designed to instantaneously notify the university community of an immediate threat or emergency situation. At least once annually, schools must test these procedures to ensure the notifications are reaching students, faculty, and staff. Connected to timely notification and warnings, universities must also investigate missing student cases within a 24 hour period of a student's unexplained absence. Moreover, schools are encouraged to adopt additional procedures and policy responses for dealing with missing student cases.

Given the concern about campus sex crime, other prominent pieces of legislation have centered on sexual victimization prevention. One provision, the Campus Sex Crime Prevention Act (CSCPA, 2000), amended the Jacob Wetterling Crimes Against Children and Sexually Violent Offender Act ("Wetterling Act"). The Wetterling Act requires states and the federal government to develop and maintain a database of all convicted sex offenders. The goal of the law is to reduce sexual victimization by providing the public with information about the whereabouts of convicted sex offenders (Mancini, 2021). Specifically, with the passage of the CSCPA, schools are required to detail where community members can find information about registered sex offenders, such as the campus police department, a local agency, or a computer network address (such as the state's online registry). The Act makes it clear that such disclosures do not violate the FERPA amendment.

VAWA/SaVE. As mentioned in Chapter 1, in 2014, the Campus Sexual Violence Elimination Act (SaVE) was adopted. It goes beyond Clery by mandating a range of provisions designed to respond to and prevent campus sex assault. Specifically, there are four goals to the Act. First, it seeks to increase *transparency*. In doing so, it expands crime statistic reporting. Recall that in accordance with the Clery Act, schools are required to publicize criminal incidents that occur on or near the campus. Under SaVE, schools must disclose a broader range of crimes occurring on campus in their annual crime statistics reports, such as intimate partner abuse, dating violence, sexual assault, and stalking. In keeping with the theme of transparency, SaVE also mandates that students or employees reporting victimization be provided with written information about the following rights:

- the option to be assisted by university authorities if reporting a crime to law enforcement
- the choice to change academic and living/working situations to avoid hostile environments
- the option to obtain or enforce a no contact directive or restraining order
- the opportunity to learn about the disciplinary review process and procedures at the institution
- the option to receive information about services for victims and survivors such as counseling, health, mental health, victim advocacy, legal assistance, and other services/programs available both on-campus and in the community

Second, the Act endeavors to ensure *accountability*. Since institutions of higher learning have the authority to judge whether sexual violations have occurred, there must be standard policies in place for disciplinary review procedures. Recall that Karjane et al.'s (2002) federal report indicates wide variation in how these processes unfold. Given this finding and the need for standardized and fair procedures, the federal government now requires that proceedings be prompt, fair, and impartial and that officials conducting them receive annual training on intimate partner abuse, sexual assault, and stalking. Additionally, SaVE states that both parties may have advocates or advisors present for disciplinary proceedings and related meetings. The institution is also charged with providing each party with written outcomes of all disciplinary proceedings.

Third, SaVE inspires to educate administrators and the university community about intimate partner and dating violence, stalking, and sexual assault. Institutions should take steps to implement primary crime prevention and awareness programs for new students, faculty, and staff; ongoing programs should also be instituted for the campus community. Additionally, SaVE instructs that universities take steps for implementing bystander intervention in preventing sexual violence and assault. Finally, to comply with the Act universities should disseminate information on risk reduction to recognize warning signs of problematic behavior.

Fourth and finally, the Act aims to forge collaborations between federal agencies, specifically, the U.S. Departments of Justice, Education, and Health and Human Services, so that best practices for preventing and responding to domestic violence, dating violence, sexual assault, and stalking on campus can be developed and implemented nationally.

Institutions determined to be in violation of the Act face a range of sanctions: official warnings from the government, the limitation or suspension of federal aid, or the loss of eligibility to participate in federal student aid programs. Furthermore, the federal government is authorized to assess fines for violations of the Act.

Nondiscrimination on the Basis of Sex ("New Rule"). On May 19, 2020, the U.S. Department of Education released a new rule that outlined several provisions to Title IX (U.S. Department of Education, 2020). Title IX refers to federal legislation enacted in 1972 that requires schools and post-secondary institutions to provide a learning environment free of sexual or gender bias (Mancini, 2021). Most of the changes were not particularly noteworthy. For example, in a review of the new rule, Sokolow (2020) explained that many are inconsequential requiring that procedural safeguards apply to both complainants (those alleging violations) and respondents (those accused of violations) involved in sexual misconduct cases (e.g., giving both parties the right to inspect documents). Having said that, some regulations are in direct contrast to earlier guidance. One provision lightens the burden of institutional accountability stressed in prior administrations. For example, the "known or should have known" definition outlined in a 2011 resource document (known as the 2011 "Dear Colleague Letter," or DCL) was replaced by a much lower standard, that of having "actual knowledge" of a violation (Brown, 2020). This lower bar is problematic, according to some observers because it could result in fewer incidents in which institutions would need to address. At the same time, the standard reduces the incidents that fall under the category of sexual harassment, in turn reducing the types of acts that institutions must address (Butler, Lee, & Fisher, 2019).

The Trump-era reforms focus heavily on "ensuring even-handed justice" (U.S. Department of Education, 2020). For example, a factsheet distributed by former U.S. Department of Education Secretary DeVos, states that the "The President's new rules will also ensure that schools can no longer inflict longstanding harm against students before providing basic, fair procedures" (U.S. Department of Education, 2020). Indeed, the Trump presidency was vocal in its criticism of the former (Obama-era) reforms. In particular, the Trump administration claimed that such reforms have resulted in "kangaroo courts," ignoring the rights of the accused (Mancini, 2021). In line with this theme, the new provisions now allow for live hearings and cross-examination (Butler et al. 2019). These are among the most controversial changes because of the concern that it could result in "double victimization," and thus retraumatize victims and survivors (Kreighbaum, 2019) or reduce reporting by those who experience sexual assault and harassment (Butler et al., 2019).

One last change concerns the use of mediation to remedy Title IX cases. Under the 2011 DCL, the U.S. Department of Education advised against the use of informal, typically non-binding resolutions like mediation, finding them to be inadequate for addressing sexual misconduct and assault (Sokolow, 2020). To be fair, the

Trump-era resolutions do include certain provisions designed to be protect complainants. That is, both parties must agree to the terms of the mediation agreement, which could include a tuition refund for victimized students, or some other informal disposition (Bauer-Wolf, 2020). Even so, some feel the mediation process does not go far enough to address what would likely be a criminal offense if tried in the justice system (Sokolow, 2020). For instance, mediation is typically a confidential process, meaning the outcome and what is agreed upon during such proceedings is not shared with the larger community. Thus, some worry that informal resolutions allow serious violations to be "swept under the rug" and worse, result in a less safe campus environment (Bauer-Wolf, 2020).

New Legislative Initiatives

Beyond these federal initiatives, other measures to address crime on campus have been proposed by some universities and advocates but not yet widely adopted nationally. These include requiring affirmative consent prior to sexual activity, the creation and development of an annual sexual victimization survey to be conducted at all universities and colleges, banning alcohol, enacting hazing legislation, and permitting students and faculty to carry concealed weapons. Given their novelty, these initiatives are discussed in detail below.

Affirmative Consent. Under Senate Bill 967, California has become one of the first states to adopt an affirmative consent standard for sexual contact (New, 2014). With the passage of the new "yes means yes" law, schools who participate in the state financial aid program are now required to uphold an affirmative consent standard in disciplinary board hearings and to educate students about the new policy. Affirmative consent moves from requiring partners to indicate unwillingness to sex ("no means no") to actively affirming all parties would like to continue engaging in sexual contact ("yes means yes"). Put differently, the affirmative consent standard mandates that all partners agree to each element of sexual conduct, through clear, verbal communication or nonverbal cues or gestures (Pugh & Becker 2018). As part of its affirmative consent standard adopted in higher education, public high schools in California are required to develop curriculum that educates students on the "yes means yes" standard and more generally, covers the topic of sexual assault (de León & Jackson, 2015). While similar bills across other jurisdictions have failed to pass, a few other states have adopted similar policies, with Vermont becoming the most recent to do so (French, 2021).

The affirmative consent legislation—seen as a way to prevent sexual victimization and hold perpetrators of it accountable—has been criticized along several dimensions. First is the concern that the law is ambiguous. For example, the precise conditions under which consent is demonstrated are left open to interpretation. That is, one sexual encounter may progress and have several stages (e.g., kissing, touching). Some have questioned how garnering consent across those various acts would work in practice (New, 2014). A second concern relates to due process. Under the California law, to avoid sanctions accused students must show that they received consent for each sexual act. Additionally, as mentioned earlier, the standard of proof for these boards, typically the preponderance of evidence standard, is a substantially lower bar than "beyond a reasonable doubt." This point is worth noting given that affirmative consent laws, so far, only apply to judicial misconduct boards and not the criminal courts. Thus, judicial boards require a higher level of consent while at the same time providing a lower standard of guilt for the accused. Given this potential lack of due process, legal experts worry that because the affirmative consent definition is inconsistent with Title IX, should accused students, if found in violation under such a standard, appeal the decision, they would likely win (Bakeman, 2015).

Campus Climate Survey. In a different direction, in recognizing that most acts of sexual victimization go unreported some have called for requiring colleges to administer an annual campus climate survey (Follingstad et al., 2020). The results could help account for the "dark figure of (sex) crime." For example, the survey could be tailored to tap specific types of assault and abuse (e.g., drug and alcohol-facilitated sex assault, sexual harassment). The results could also be used to inform efforts to prevent sexual violence on campus and respond to victims' needs. If institutions find that students are unaware of the various resources available to them, for instance, outreach could be improved and better targeted (Mancini, 2021).

Alcohol Ban. Still post-secondary schools have pursued other avenues for preventing crime, such as limiting the availability of alcohol on campus (Trangenstein, Wall, & Jernigan, 2019). The logic for the change stems from the presumption that a reduction in alcohol consumption may reduce the incidence of certain crimes, particularly, sexual violence, harassment, and other forms of interpersonal violence. In 2015, Dartmouth College gained national prominence for instituting a ban on hard liquor in its quest to reduce such harmful behavior (Sanburn, 2015). One year later, Stanford University proposed a similar measure (Reilly, 2016) and since then other universities have followed in that direction (Field, 2018). There may be less opposition to the bans given that student populations report drinking less in recent years compared to earlier cohorts, with one-quarter reporting not drinking at all (McCabe et al., 2020). Even so, the prohibitions, as of now, apply only to select universities.

Hazing Legislation. As previously reviewed, a significant number of college students will personally experience a hazing incident and a majority reporting being aware of acts of hazing that occur on campus. Since the first edition of this text, over five years ago, an increasing number of states have considered or have enacted anti-hazing laws. As of 2021, 44 of 50 states have adopted anti-hazing laws, although there is wide variation in the breadth and strength of the laws (StopHazing, 2021). For example, in Virginia and other states hazing acts are considered misdemeanor offenses, meaning the sanctions associated with such crimes are relatively minor, such as community service or a fine (Thompson, 2021). Given the gravity of such incidents, there are efforts to increase the punishment associated with hazing crimes. To illustrate, the parents of a student who allegedly died from hazing at Virginia Commonwealth University, Adam Oakes, have lobbied the Virginia General Assembly for tougher sanctioning (Thompson, 2021).

Additionally, a bipartisan Congressional bill, the Report and Educate About Campus Hazing (REACH) Act was recently introduced by federal lawmakers (Hendrix, 2021). Its goal is two-fold. It seeks to require post-secondary institutions to report known hazing incidents as part of the annual Clery report. Moreover, it would require colleges to implement anti-hazing education for students. At the time of this writing, the REACH Act has not yet been adopted at the federal level (Hendrix, 2021).

Concealed Carry. With the substantial media and public attention given to mass shootings (Schildkraut, Elsass, & Meredith 2018), some policymakers have proposed permitting campus carry on college campuses. All 50 states allow citizens to carry concealed weapons so long as they abide by the specific statute (e.g., receive special permit; National Conference of State Legislatures, 2019). However, 16 states, such as California, Illinois, and Florida have specifically banned students, faculty, staff, and visitors from possessing concealed weapons on campus. In contrast, 23 other states including Virginia, Alabama, Indiana, and Maryland leave the decision to permit or ban up to the individual university or college. As of 2019, only a small minority of states, seven, such as Arkansas, Colorado, Utah, and Idaho, have provisions that permit concealed weapons on campus (National Conference of State Legislatures, 2019). According to a national review of campus carry laws (National Conference of State Legislatures, 2019), Tennessee—not included in this list of permitting states—has a unique statute in that it only permits concealed carry among faculty (excluding students and visitors to campus).

It is arguably the most controversial of the new efforts discussed. Proponents of carry rights argue that the laws have great utility in preventing crime (McMahon-Howard, Scherer, & McCafferty, 2020). Put simply, advocates promote the idea of "defensive gun use" (DGU). The idea assumes that DGU may result in deterrence if potential shooters, to the extent that they spend time planning the attack, are aware that citizens are also armed. On a different front, in an instance of an active shooting, armed students and staff could potentially turn the tables on the perpetrators, reducing the number of casualties and injuries. Although permitting guns on campus might engender greater DGU by the university community in the instance of an active shooter, it is also possible, per detractors of the policy, that concealed carry could result in unintended effects (Mancini, Cook, Smith, & McDougle, 2020). For instance, there is the concern that the gun could go off accidently in a crowded classroom or populated area of the campus. Another worry is that students who carry might use the gun against a professor or fellow student in a fit of rage.

To be sure, these five efforts—affirmative consent laws, mandatory climate surveys, drinking bans, hazing legislation, and gun carry laws are controversial and because of their relative novelty, it is unclear whether they will effectively reduce campus violence over long periods of time. Still, their development illustrates the national and on-going focus on responding to college crime.

Educational Programs

The above section described new and some controversial policies to respond to campus crime. However, one crime prevention effort that has enjoyed a longer tenure is educational initiatives. We would of course expect institutions of higher learning to encourage such measures. These programs fit into four broad categories: alcohol awareness, sexual assault prevention, property protection, and active shooter training.

As mentioned previously, there is some indication that alcohol use among students may have declined compared to earlier cohorts, with one in four reporting not drinking at all. Even so, the latest federal statistics, from a survey of self-reported drinking use, found that problematic drinking still occurs. On any given year 33 percent of full-time college students (ages 18 to 22) report at least one episode of "binge drinking" (having several drinks across a short period of time) and 9 percent fit criteria for having an "alcohol use disorder," or problems regulating their alcohol use (National Institute on Alcohol Abuse and Alcoholism, 2021). With increased concern about underage drinking, many incoming college students are now required to complete a course about alcohol awareness. To illustrate, in one study of nearly 800 university administrators, Wechsler, Seibring, Liu, and Ahl (2004) revealed that over 80 percent felt drinking was either a "major problem" or "problem" on their campus. For this reason, most colleges have mandatory alcohol awareness program in place (see later, Carey, Scott-Sheldon, Garey, Elliott, & Carey, 2016). Many of these programs target groups presumed to be at risk of drinking, such as for first-year students, fraternity or sorority members, and athletes (Wechsler et al., 2004). These programs focus on a range of issues such as educating students about the effects of alcohol on behavior and health, dangers of alcohol use, and strategies to address alcohol dependence (Welsh, Shentu, & Sarvey, 2019).

Sexual assault prevention is another priority on college campuses given the prevalence and the consequences of sexual violence on student health and academic performance (Mancini & Budd, 2020). These programs are designed to educate students about risk factors, consent standards, resources for those who are victimized or know others in need of assistance, and other aspects of sex crime prevention. Some universities mandate that students complete a course designed to tackle these issues (Zapp, Buelow, Soutiea, Berkowitz, & DeJong, 2021). In another direction, some institutions offer rape aggression and defense (RAD) classes that aim to teach students how best to physically protect themselves from perpetrators (Mancini & Budd, 2020). A recent initiative, bystander intervention, has also been developed to respond to sexual violence. Research indicates that many people wrestle with what they should do when observing incidents that have the potential to escalate to crimes (Coker, Bush, Fisher, Swan, Williams, Clear, & DeGue, 2016). Bystander intervention (BI) training centers on providing third-parties with assistance in identifying these situations and tips to deescalate the situation. Because BI has become a key initiative universities have explored to prevent sexual violence, we will talk more about its efficacy, and also the distinction between BI and general educational efforts, in the next section, "Research-Driven Initiatives for Crime Prevention on Campus."

Colleges and universities are also hot spots for property crime. One large multi-state study found that larceny offenses were the most commonly reported campus victimization (Fisher et al., 1998). These offenses include theft of personal property and individuals' identities. This risk stems in part from the nature of the college lifestyle (Mustaine & Tewksbury, 1998; Reyns et al., 2021). Students, particularly freshmen, often live in close quarters with roommates whom they may have just met. In a typical dormitory, there are many common areas, late-night parties where property is left unattended, and a vast array of small, portable electronics and goods. Not least, students may share laptops or other devices that contain sensitive information such as credit card information or social security numbers. For these reasons, colleges and universities may offer or encourage students to use property protection services. These "target-hardening" efforts include personalizing property, such as laptops and smartphones, using bike locks and dorm safes, preventing identify theft by securing personal data, and purchasing insurance in the event that property is stolen (Hoak, 2012). Additionally, most students living on campus may be required to use their student identification card or unique pin for access to dormitories (Abramson, 2004). Student resident advisors employed by the institution may also serve as "capable guardians" in preventing property crime by monitoring the security of on campus housing (Fromme, Corbin, & Kruse, 2008). As part of safety campaigns on campus, students are asked to always follow instructions to keep dorms and their personal property secure—for instance, by not propping doors or leaving their property unattended in common areas like the library (Shellenbarger, 2005). Not least, most universities report installing some type of surveillance system in residence halls and around campus buildings to deter crime, including property offenses (Abramson, 2004; Liedka, Meehan, & Lauer, 2019).

Universities and colleges nationwide have also wrestled with how to most effectively respond to active shooters (Peterson, Sackrison, & Polland, 2015). As Fox and Savage (2009, p. 1466) note, the term has been used by institutions to "characterize the perpetrator of a seemingly random assault with a firearm." Fortunately, mass shootings at universities, although widely publicized, are incredibly rare events (Schildkraut et al., 2018). One report published by the Federal Bureau of Investigation (Drysdale, Modzeleski, & Simons, 2010) analyzing campus crime statistics from 2005 to 2008 indicates that less than 45 homicide offenses involving college students occur annually. In comparison, during this same time frame, 3,460 sex offenses, 4,975 robberies, and 5,418 aggravated assaults were committed annually against college students, faculty, or staff (see for a later report indicating a similar trend, National Center for Education Statistics, 2020b). Hence, relative to other violent interpersonal offenses, homicides are unlikely to occur on our nation's college campuses. Even so, one death on campus is one too many. Thus, in response to growing concern about campus shootings over the last decade colleges have responded by mandating or encouraging incoming students to complete active shooter training (Myers, 2017). The courses are designed to inform students about how to spot potentially dangerous individuals on campus, techniques to stay safe during a mass shooting, and resources for those concerned about troubled students, faculty, or staff.

Because crime prevention is an important topic, we will talk more about these initiatives and their empirical efficacy in the following section, "Research-Driven Initiatives for Crime Prevention on Campus." For now, this section can be summarized as indicating the specialized types of educational efforts that seek to inform the campus community about crime prevention.

Victim Services

Up until this point, our discussion has revolved around laws and efforts to prevent and address offending on campus. How do universities respond to the needs of campus crime victims? What programs and policies exist for those affected by campus crime? The answer, of course, depends on the institution. However, with the implementation of federal legislation, such as the Clery Act and Title IX, post-secondary schools have implemented numerous victim assistance and support programs. For example, 24 hour psychiatric and mental health services for victims, crisis hot lines, assistance with reporting crimes and obtaining restraining and no-contact orders, and employment (e.g., modifying work schedule) and academic accommodations (permitting students to drop courses, receive extensions for school work) are illustrative of efforts to help victims of campus crime (Office for Civil Rights, 2015).

© Luis Molinero/Shutterstock.com

There are concerns, though, that these services are not reaching victims of campus crime. Student awareness of the types of services and support is low. For example, one investigation of students attending an unnamed university in the South found a majority, over 60 percent, were unaware of the range of services available to them should they become victims of crime (Franklin, Menaker, & Jin, 2019). A larger, national study of college students found that less than 20 percent of crime victims seek victims services (Sinozich & Langton, 2014). The last wave of the AAU CCS, the large-scale campus climate survey discussed in Chapter 1, found similarly low percentages, with only 15 percent of students who have experienced a sexual assault or misconduct incident reporting they sought help or services (Cantor et al., 2019). For this reason, advocates suggest that to improve usage rates post-secondary institutions (and other agencies that serve victims of sex assault) should consider the voices and input of survivors of sexual violence in designing outreach efforts (Kirkner, Lorenz, & Ullman, 2021).

Reflection   **4**

Victim Services

Are you aware of your institution's victim programs and services? What agency distributes them? Do you feel students are likely to use them? If not, why? Are there ways they could be improved to reach a wider population?

Up until this juncture, our discussion has centered on responses to criminal victimization. We now move toward outlining research-supported ways you can protect yourself from crime while attending college. Before exploring this new unit, be sure to check out the Chapter 2 Exercise for further reinforcement of key concepts.

How Well Do You Know . . .

Students are typically surprised to discover the many laws and policies designed to protect them on campus. Think about the statements below and determine if they are true or false based on what we have covered in Chapter 2. If you detect false statements, explain why the statements are inaccurate. The web links below reinforce these concepts.

http://www.bjs.gov/index.cfm?ty=tp&tid=76
https://www2.ed.gov/admins/lead/safety/campus.html
http://knowyourix.org/
understanding-the-campus-save-act/
https://stophazing.org/policy/state-laws/

1. Because of shrinking budgets, most colleges have decreased their reliance on campus law enforcement.

   If false, why?

2. Typically, disciplinary review boards require that institutions prove "beyond a reasonable doubt" that a violation of the student conduct code occurred.

   If false, why?

3. The Jeanne Clery Act provides certain institutions—specifically those that have demonstrated "best practices" in reporting of campus crime—to be exempt from disclosing the extent of reported victimization.

   If false, why?

4. The Campus Sex Crime Prevention Act (CSCPA, 2000) requires that colleges and universities include information regarding registered sex offenders who may be attending or otherwise affiliated with the institution.

   If false, why?

5. The Campus Sexual Violence Elimination (SaVE) Act seeks to increase protections such as providing schedule accommodations for victims of sexual offenses.

   If false, why?

6. The Nondiscrimination on the Basis of Sex Policy enacted under President Trump sought to address concerns that former federal guidance reduced due process for respondents or students accused of sexual assault.

   If false, why?

7. Currently, federal law mandates that public universities provide anti-hazing education and training to incoming college students.

   If false, why

Research-Driven Initiatives for Crime Prevention on Campus

3

1. What theories are helpful for explaining campus crime?

2. What are the major premises behind the routine activity theory?

3. How do lifestyle characteristics influence victimization risk among students?

4. What does the victimization precipitation theory assume about victimization and crime?

5. What research-supported strategies for crime prevention exist?

LEARNING GOALS

- To evaluate how crime theories can be used to understand campus victimization.
- To compare and contrast theoretical perspectives that apply to crime and violence on campus.
- To be familiar with crime prevention efforts.

Criminologists have developed several theories of victimization risk. In turn, the theories are useful for designing crime prevention efforts. What follows is first a discussion about three prominent theories of offending and victimization relevant to the higher education context: the routine activities theory, lifestyle theory, and victim precipitation theory. Afterward, our focus shifts to research driven prevention policies and practices. By becoming aware of the risk factors associated with criminal victimization (and empirically-supported crime prevention efforts), you will be better aware of potentially dangerous situations and how to avoid them.

Theories of Offending and Victimization—Routine Activity Theory

Three theories appear particularly relevant toward explaining campus crime. The routine activity theory (RAT) was developed by Felson and Cohen (1979). The theorists observed that from 1947 to 1974 predatory crimes increased dramatically, particularly during the 1960s. In explaining this crime shift, Felson and Cohen (1979) argued that changes in Americans' daily routines were to blame. For instance, over this time period, homes, once guarded by women were more likely to be vacant during the day as females began to enter the workforce in large numbers. Also during this time frame, once clunky electronic goods, like large televisions and radios, were transformed into slimmer, and hence, portable and easily movable versions. These changes in turn, created new opportunities for victimization. Specifically, the theory argues that crime occurs when three factors—motivated offenders, availability of suitable targets, and absence of capable guardians—converge in time and space. In many ways, the first criterion—the presence of motivated offenders—can be readily assumed. That is, under the rational choice perspective, the framework upon which routine activity theory derives, all individuals have the propensity to commit crime; what constrains deviant behavior is the prospect of experiencing pain (e.g., detection, punishment) arising from the criminal act (Rosenfeld & Messner, 2013). The second condition, suitable targets, refers to unguarded goods and vulnerable individuals. For example, a smartphone forgotten in a bathroom stall would fit Felson and Cohen's (1979) conception of a suitable target. The item is easily transportable, valuable, and unattended.

The third and final element, absence of capable guardians, refers to instances where no competent person or thing is available to detect or impede an offense. Under this perspective, law enforcement officers, security guards, neighbors, and teachers are illustrative of entities that could report or intervene during a criminal act. Additionally, the theory stipulates that capable guardianship extends beyond people. Animals, such as guard dogs, and even things, like security systems, also function as crime discouragers.

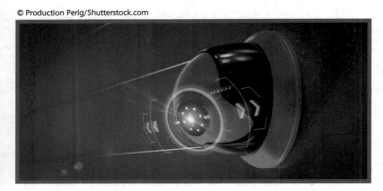

© Production Perig/Shutterstock.com

How does this theory translate to understanding college crime? As advised by routine activity theorists, we should assume motivated offenders always exist, even on the relatively safest of college campuses. The presence of suitable targets, the second condition of the theory, clearly exists on the average institution. National data indicate nearly all students own at least one portable electronic device (Chen, Seilhamer, Bennett, & Bauer, 2015). Thus, a large supply of attractive, easily movable, and unguarded goods exists for property offenders. Moreover, a person (perhaps intoxicated or alone) would also qualify as a "suitable target" for experiencing interpersonal crime. A motivated offender might evaluate a target as "suitable" (and hence, at risk for victimization) if that person is alone, or perhaps intoxicated. Although not all college students drink or engage in drug use, a substantial proportion do (National Center on Addiction and Substance Abuse, 2007; Schulenberg et al., 2020; Wechsler et al., 2004); this factor, in turn indicates that a wide pool of possible targets exist on the typical college campus. Finally, the lack of capable guardianship comes into play. Although college campuses are busy places, they are not always well guarded. Property is often left unattended at various areas on campus (recall all those signs in the library and campus buildings warning students to supervise their property?). Dorm rooms and the property inside them (suitable targets) are not always supervised by resident assistants (RAs) or other students (Shellenbarger, 2005). Accordingly, as these two scenarios illustrate a motivated offender has few obstacles to overcome to steal unguarded property. Lack of capable guardianship has implications for not just property offenses, but other serious interpersonal crimes as well. Students may engage in sexual relationships and these experiences often occur in private (Hirsch & Khan, 2020). Thus, under this context in the case of an intoxicated person (i.e., a suitable target) and an offender motivated to sexually assault that person, there may not be a capable guardian available to intervene. To conclude this section, RAT provides a theoretical framework for explaining patterns of property and violent victimization among college students.

© William Perugini/Shutterstock.com

Theories of Offending and Victimization—Lifestyle Theory

A second theoretical perspective relevant toward understanding campus crime is the lifestyle theory. Over sixty years ago, Marvin Wolfgang became one of the first criminologists to uncover that a criminal lifestyle influenced later homicide victimization (1957) and robbery risk (Wolfgang & Singer, 1978). His discovery has been explained under the phenomenon of the "victim-offender" overlap. Subsequent studies (Broidy, Daday, Crandall, Sklar, & Jost, 2006; Dobrin, 2001; Pizarro, Zgoba, & Jennings, 2011) including a large meta-analysis (Jennings, Piquero, & Reingle, 2012), or a study of all published studies in a specific area, have demonstrated that criminal lifestyles significantly increase the probability of being victimized at a later point in time.

To be clear, college students' lifestyles differ in many ways from the "criminal lifestyle" identified by Wolfgang and later colleagues. Indeed, college students have unique habits and characteristics that are distinct from many other social and demographic groups. For instance, the typical college student lives on or attends school on campuses that house large numbers of young, unsupervised people. This is an important observation given that crime is a young person's game. That is, criminological research reveals that younger age is predictive of a higher victimization risk *and* offending propensity (Siegel, 2018). Thus, having a community with many young people increases the potential pool of victims and perpetrators.

Beyond this characteristic, college students tend to be social. Engaging in recreational activities, going out at night, and being part of social organizations (e.g., fraternities, student clubs) are typical experiences for the average student in the U.S. To illustrate, on any given year, nine million college students will join a fraternity or sorority (Glass, 2012). Similarly, most college students admit to "partying" at least once a week. A large online poll (N = 1,147) conducted by Pedersen and LaBrie (2007) found that men reported an average of 5.19 party days (i.e., days where alcohol was consumed in the last month in a social setting) whereas females reported slightly less but still substantial, 5.15 party days. This same study showed that many students—nearly two-thirds—"pre-party" or engage in drinking prior to the main event. Taking shots of liquor (67 percent and 90 percent for males and females, respectively) and beer (80 percent and 43 percent for males and females, respectively) were the most frequently reported pre-party activities. More recently, there is evidence that students are "partying" less than in earlier years (Giambrone, 2015). Additionally, indicating the dwindling appeal of the party lifestyle, a large percentage of students—nearly 80 percent—reported that they would be willing to forgo partying in the wake of the COVID-19 pandemic (Rothschild, 2020). Even so, many social occasions during the college experience involve heavy drinking (Wechsler et al., 2004), and to a lesser extent, drug use (National Center on Addiction and Substance Abuse, 2007; Weiss & Dilks, 2016). While it is true that the COVID-19 pandemic changed habits and lifestyles, including those of college students, it is likely that most students will resume their typical lifestyle as restrictions are lifted and life returns to normal for most communities.

How then might the typical lifestyle of students affect their victimization risk? According to the lifestyle theory, the confluence of college-related factors—a large concentration of younger individuals, mostly unsupervised and living in close proximity to others, social activities, and drinking and drug use—create a perfect storm in enabling victimization. Indeed, there are several pathways by which lifestyle affects crime risk. For instance, students, many of whom are young and on their own for the first time, may simply be unaware of safety dangers. They might not lock doors regularly, may fail to guard their property, or may be too trusting of others. Because of their limited experience of living on their own, students may ascribe to a "false sense of security," believing that since college campuses are generally secure, they need not take the proper precautions to ensure their safety. While social engagements are important (and fun!) features of college, they too enhance one's risk for victimization. Social engagements often occur in the evening, a time when crime risk increases (Baum & Klaus, 2005). Not least, alcohol and drug use often accompany these social activities. This point is critical to highlight given that prior research has linked being impaired to increased victimization among college students (Hirsch & Khan, 2000; Fisher et al., 1998; Fisher et al., 2000). Additionally, as referenced earlier, being involved in crime, such as the drug trade (that is, purchasing and selling illegal substances) is generally linked with greater levels of victimization, a phenomenon criminologists have dubbed the "victim-offender" overlap (Wolfgang, 1957; Jennings et al., 2012). Such illicit behavior typically occurs in secret and offenders might specifically target "deviant others," perhaps believing they are unlikely to report victimization given their own criminal actions. There are other pathways by which substance use and abuse can affect victimization. Using alcohol to excess or drugs lowers one's use of protective measures and may also signal to offenders that the victim is physically vulnerable.

It is not just alcohol and drug use that may expose students to crime. Reyns and Scherer (2018) in an analysis of over 43,000 college students reported that two prosocial engagements, specifically, volunteering and employment, which frequently involve interacting with a variety of individuals, were associated with an increased likelihood of experiencing victimization, specifically, stalking offenses. This of course does not mean that students should not pursue such important milestones, but namely, they should be aware that any social engagement carries some risk of interacting with individuals who may perpetrate crimes against them. In short, the college lifestyle may invite opportunities to be victimized by others.

Theories of Offending and Victimization—Victim Precipitation Theory

The third theoretical perspective is complementary but distinct from the earlier two theories. This framework argues that victims' actions may contribute to the progression of a criminal event. The theory is not intended to "victim blame" or unfairly attribute responsibility to crime victims, but rather attempts, from a behavioral or criminological standpoint, to identify factors related to the initiation of crime. According to the theory, two types of victim precipitation exist. The first, active precipitation, refers to instances where victims may act provocatively, using "fighting words" or acting in an aggressive fashion (Siegel, 2018). The second classification, passive precipitation, occurs when victims possess some characteristic—perhaps unknowingly—that threatens the perpetrators or encourages the offense (Daly & Wilson, 1988).

How does this perspective apply to college crime? Let us first consider an example depicting active precipitation. According to theorists (Siegel, 2018), active precipitation refers to instances where victims directly antagonize or threaten a potential offender. Perhaps two students who have opposing allegiance to a sports team exchange heated words in a college bar. The victim (and the first to start the "debate") is then punched in the nose by the aggrieved offender. Under the precipitation theory, the victim's initial jawing is illustrative of "active" precipitation since it is a direct affront to the perpetrator. It could be presumed that speaking negatively about one's sports team might create tension among others who have an allegiance to that team. Here again, the emphasis is not to place blame on the victimized parties, but to understand their behavior as part of a sequence of events leading to crime.

How does passive precipitation differ from active precipitation? Recall that passive precipitation indicates an indirect "affront" or threatening or competing behavior. That is, victims may hold some characteristic (perhaps unsuspectingly) that incites violence from offenders. We can turn to this hypothetical scenario: Two students compete for a major part in their university play. One student, the superior actor, lands the part and the other student, angry and jealous about losing it, vows revenge. To be sure, the "winning" student did not taunt or otherwise provoke the offender; however, the perpetrator perceives the situation as highly unfair and the victim as deserving of harm and responds by hurting her competition. To summarize, the victim precipitation theory assumes that the victims' actions either directly (active precipitation) or indirectly (passive precipitation) precede a criminal event. Snapshot Summary Box 6 compares and contrasts the major themes of each theory.

© Sin314/Shutterstock.com

Research Evaluating Crime Prevention

Now that we have outlined theoretical perspectives of campus crime, we move to discussing prevention efforts that have been studied by criminologists. There are four that we focus on: target hardening strategies, drug and alcohol use education, cyber safety initiatives, and sexual assault prevention efforts. Although this list is not

Snapshot Summary

6   **Summary of Campus Victimization Theories**

Theory	Major Concepts	Cause of Crime	Implications
Routine Activities	Capable guardianship; suitable targets; motivated offenders	Crime occurs when capable guardianship is absent or weak and suitable targets are present (motivated offenders assumed)	Strengthen capable guardianship; reduce availability of easy targets (e.g., unsupervised goods or vulnerable persons)
Lifestyle	Daily habits; victim-offender overlap; college lifestyle as risky	The probability of victimization increases as engagement in risky or deviant activities increases	Reduce behaviors associated with risk (e.g., drug and alcohol use) and educate victims about potentially risky habits and behaviors
Victim Precipitation	Active precipitation; passive precipitation	Active precipitation refers to victim behavior that may directly provoke or anger offender; passive precipitation occurs when victims unknowingly share a trait that makes them appear vulnerable	Suggest victims disengage in situations that could potentially become heated or dangerous (e.g., football game)

exhaustive, it is inclusive of the major efforts undertaken by institutions of higher learning to reduce campus victimization.

Target Hardening. As hit upon earlier, target hardening refers to efforts to secure the safety of property or individuals. This goal can be accomplished in many ways. For instance, by increasing the risk of detection and apprehension of the offender, it follows that offenders may think twice about committing say, theft offenses or interpersonal violence. Additionally, target hardening can refer to incorporating measures to "harden" or secure a target—that is, by making it more difficult or inconvenient to commit crime.

It is recognized that certain locations of an area, "hot spots," may be more susceptible to crime than others. As we reviewed earlier, national data indicate that violent victimizations against college students were concentrated in open areas, parking garages, and private residences (Baum & Klaus, 2005). In an investigation studying crime at a major comprehensive public university in the U.S., Robinson and his colleague (2007) sought to identify hot spots on campus using spatial or mapping analysis. In particular, Robinson and Roh (2007) relied on official data, or crimes known to law enforcement. Results from this examination revealed that drug and alcohol violations, property offenses (e.g., breaking and entering, vandalism, theft), assaults, harassment crimes, and sex offenses (forcible fondling) were concentrated primarily at or near on-campus student housing. In contrast, another "hot spot" included high-traffic areas. These locations were described as highly traveled areas between the main parts of campus (e.g., near educational buildings and parking areas). According to the analysis, these areas experienced a "moderate" amount of crimes. Notably, the offenses appeared relevant to the location. For instance, thefts, vandalism, and offenses against automobiles (e.g., hit and runs) were significantly more likely to occur in these locations compared to other places on campus. The study is important for demonstrating that policies designed to prevent campus crime should account for spatial variation in victimization. Extending this focus on place, McGrath, Perumean-Chaney, and Sloan (2014) found that areas or "nodes" of campus more heavily traveled experienced higher rates of crime. Specifically, using the University of Alabama-Birmingham (UAB) as a case study McGrath and colleagues (2014) reported that property crime was significantly higher on the medical center side of UAB, concentrated within a 14-block radius, than around other areas of campus. The researchers apply the routine activities theory we previously discussed to contextualize their results, explaining that "the constant traffic 24 hours per day, seven days per week within this medical center appears to provide an activity space that intersects potential offenders and victims that result in higher instances of property crimes" (McGrath et al., 2014, p. 277).

Other research has pointed to "hot times" in which crime is more likely to occur. In a study analyzing variation in crime trends at a large public university, Nobles and his associates (2010) found that most on-campus arrests occurred on Saturdays (with or without a college football game). Additionally, college students were significantly more likely to be arrested during the weekends (Thursdays through Saturdays), rather than during other times of the week (see also Jennings, Gover, & Pudrzynska, 2007). In explaining this finding, Nobles et al. (2010) reason that among college students the earlier portion of the week is devoted to low-risk activities, or factors that typically inhibit crime—studying and attending classes, for instance. However, the latter part of the week invites greater opportunities to socialize and engage in drug and alcohol use, particularly off-campus; accordingly, a larger supply of victims and potential perpetrators interact during this time frame. Bolstering this hypothesis are NCVS findings that violent victimizations against college students are more likely to occur in the evening rather than during the day (Baum & Klaus, 2005). In short, both place and *time* may be relevant factors to consider when designing campus crime prevention policies.

Generally, research suggests that individuals who practice aspects of target hardening particularly in "hot spots," and presumably at "hot times" are less likely to be victimized. For example, in a classic study analyzing crime patterns among 3,472 college students, distinguished criminologist Bonnie Fisher and her colleagues (1998) demonstrated that students who incorporated target hardening into their daily lives (e.g., routinely ask others to "watch their stuff") had reduced odds of experiencing property theft victimization.

Following the target hardening logic, institutions have incorporated numerous measures to ensure public safety. To illustrate, the iconic "blue lights" that you have probably seen on campus act as alarm systems and are activated when someone presses the "help" button (Aisenberg, 2011). When this happens, the lights are illuminated and an alarm sounds. Security is subsequently dispatched to the location. The lights are placed strategically throughout campus—in areas where students congregate and where crime is perceived to occur, or "hot spots" (Fisher, 1995). Presumably, because the lights operate 24 hours a day, 7 days a week, they are accessible at any time, particularly during "hot times"—instances where crime may peak (e.g., the weekends and in the evenings) or when there are fewer capable guardians on campus.

Despite the initial appeal of these lights, some have questioned their efficacy and in doing so, have called for other options (Kozlowski, 2013). For example, one critique is that the blue lights are rarely used and their efficacy in preventing crime has not been assessed. Indeed, one recent survey of students attending the University of Mary Washington in Virginia (N = 301) found that only 1 percent reported using the

blue lights for an emergency (Ratti, 2010). It appears much more common for students to use the phones for non-emergencies rather than to seek help during a threatening situation (e.g., students calling to ask for assistance fixing a flat tire; see generally, Kozlowski, 2013).

Another concern is that the call boxes are outdated. Since virtually all students have access to smartphones, apps downloaded on users' phones might more effectively dispatch help to those in need (Yabe, 2017). Indeed, since the last publication of this text, institutional interest in developing such apps has increased substantially (Yabe, 2017). Currently, LiveSafe, an app co-developed by Kristina Anderson, a campus safety advocate who survived the Virginia Tech shooting in 2007 (Hoover, 2017), is used throughout the U.S. (Barr, 2018).

Recall that place and time are important considerations in tailoring other campus crime prevention programs. For this reason, colleges nationwide have incorporated other measures, such as providing security escorts for faculty, staff, and students concerned about traveling on campus, particularly during the evening hours. In line with blue lights, these programs are also illustrative of "target hardening." Escorts act as capable guardians and accompany potentially vulnerable targets across campus during potentially dangerous times (at night). Under this logic, it is substantially more difficult (and inconvenient) for potential offenders to victimize such targets. Few studies have evaluated whether such services are associated with a reduction in crime. However, some work indicates that these may be largely ineffective as students do not typically take advantage of them. For example, in her study of awareness and use of popular campus crime prevention policies, Ratti (2010) discovered that only 14 percent of students had ever used police escort services during their enrollment. In a later analysis, college students rated escort services as being among the "least helpful" campus safety services available to them (Merianos, King, & Vidourek, 2017). Accordingly, these initiatives might be improved by increasing their appeal or by making them easier to use.

Reflection 5

Target Hardening

Think about the last time you practiced a form of target hardening. What (or whom) were you protecting? Was the practice successful?

Substance Abuse Education. Because drug and alcohol use may impair victims and potentially incite violence, campuses nationwide have incorporated substance abuse education into the curriculum (Wechsler, Nelson, Lee, Seibring, Lewis, & Keeling, 2003). Some include it as a substantive topic under orientation or a first year experience course. Many students may not be completely aware of the negative effects of alcohol and drugs, including its link to poor academic performance, health problems, and criminal victimization. For example, the National Council on Alcoholism and Drug Dependence (2015) estimates that every year approximately 5,000 young people under the age of 21 die as a result of underage drinking. Over half of these deaths, 3,500 are criminally induced—arising from homicide offenses or drunk driving. Significantly less, 300, are determined to be suicides, and the remainder involves injuries such as falls, burns, and drowning.

Does educating students about these risks and other facets of substance abuse prevent future problematic drinking? The answer, based on published research indicates that overall programs designed to educate students about substance use and abuse are linked with a reduction in the occurrence of negative outcomes. For example, a large meta-analysis examining 62 studies published from 1985 to 2007 that used random assignment to evaluate the impact of substance abuse awareness programs demonstrated that students who participated in risk reduction interventions drank significantly less relative to controls (Carey, Scott-Sheldon, Carey, & DeMartini, 2007). Additionally, the study found that students who had completed interventions also reported fewer alcohol-related problems (e.g., drinking and driving, property damage, fights, alcohol poisoning) over longer periods of time. However, the "type" of intervention mattered. Carey and her colleagues (2007) revealed that individual, face-to-face interventions using motivational techniques and personalized normative feedback (e.g., dispelling misperceptions about substance use) were associated with the greatest reduction alcohol-related problems. The emphasis on random assignment is relevant because studies that randomly assign subjects to the experimental or control group are considered more valid than studies that do not use randomization (Campbell & Stanley, 1963). Thus, the Carey et al. (2007) seminal meta-analysis represents compelling support for educational initiatives to decrease substance abuse among college students.

A later meta-analysis also sought to understand the impact of university-delivered alcohol and substance abuse education. It identified 88 studies, with most focused on addressing alcohol use (Plotnikoff, Costigan, Kennedy, Robards, Germov, & Wildd, 2019). Overall, education served to reduce problematic drinking. Similar to Carey et al. (2007), the review also identified "best practices" in developing educational initiatives. Specifically, dynamic and interactive (e.g., face-to-face) modes of education appear most beneficial in reducing problematic behavior among students. While the Plotnikoff et al. (2019) review suggests positive benefits of education, it cautions that fewer interventions have tested the impact of education on drug and substance abuse (beyond alcohol). The authors recommend a greater level of scrutiny for those interventions.

Cyber Safety Efforts. With the advent of the Internet, cyber-related victimization is increasingly becoming a concern nationally, and particularly among youthful populations, such as college students (Finn, 2004; Wick et al., 2017). Cyber crimes fit into two broad classifications. These offenses comprise a range of interpersonal violations such as cyber bullying, harassment, and stalking. In contrast, cyber-related offenses may also include property crimes like fraudulent credit card use or identity theft. With this realization, institutions of higher learning have incorporated measures such as requiring secure passwords for logging into university accounts, creating departments that assist with cyber threats and Internet-technology crimes, and general education about online risks such as identity theft.

Although little research has evaluated the impact of many of these prevention efforts (Jones, Mitchell, & Walsh, 2014) a handful of studies provide some support for the potential of education to reduce victimization. As an example, the i-SAFE program was created to promote online safety for young people by informing them about intellectual property rights, identity theft, and other risks of online dangers (e.g., harassment and sexual predators). In a federally funded investigation of the program, Chinbill, Leicht, and Lunghofer (2006) using a quasi-experimental design, found that in comparison to middle school students who did not participate, attitudes about Internet safety (e.g., knowledge about Internet predators, awareness of intellectual property laws) were substantially improved among the students who completed the course; however, there was no evidence that risky Internet behavior (e.g., downloading copyrighted material without paying for it, providing personal information to strangers) changed after exposure to the program. A similar program, NetSmartz, developed by the Boys and Girls Clubs of America and National Center for Missing and Exploited Children shares similar goals to the i-SAFE program (Branch Associates, 2002). Specifically, it seeks to educate youths (6 to 18 years old) about how to recognize and respond to potential Internet risks. In line with the earlier i-SAFE evaluation, results from an outcome study suggest that attitudes and general awareness of participants significantly improved compared to controls. Additionally, although there was no evidence that problematic behaviors were reduced in the experimental group, over 75 percent of participants reported that they would make better choices in the future that would reduce their risk for cyber victimization. One later study of college students determined a comprehensive module improved knowledge of risks of phishing, identity theft, and other forms of cyber-victimization among both computer science and non-computer science majors (Peker, Ray, Da Silva, Gibson, & Lamberson, 2016).

Notwithstanding this positive result, earlier evaluations indicate that while some types of programming increases awareness among students, knowledge of risk does not always translate into behavior change. A recent review of prior educational efforts suggests that the relative inefficacy of some interventions may be due to a misalignment of many past efforts and the reality of cyber-victimization among young people (Finkelhor, Walsh, Jones, Mitchell, & Collier, 2020). For example, Finklehor and colleagues (2020) explain that cyberbullying and harassment can occur in the "offline" environment as well as the virtual one. Thus, one recommendation proposed is to change the design of many cyber-education modules, which tend to only address virtual forms of victimization (e.g., Peker et al., 2016). Another is to examine how college students respond to cybersecurity training. Much of the published work in this area evaluates the impact of education on younger populations (Finkelhor et al., 2020), although there are exceptions (Peker et al., 2016). While it is critical to start education early, a continued focus on

college students, particularly concerning university-based interventions, is needed (Jones et al., 2014). Like many interventions, it is clear that the design, target population, and duration of the initiative determine the efficacy of cyber-crime prevention programming.

Sexual Assault Prevention. As discussed earlier, sexual victimization is prevalent on college and university campuses nationwide (Mancini, 2021). As federal data indicate, college students are significantly less likely to report sexual victimization to a campus official or law enforcement agency (Sinozich & Langton, 2014). For these reasons, greater attention has been given to developing and implementing programs and policies that address sexual assault on campus. Some notable prevention strategies implemented nationally include: self defense and assertiveness training, bystander intervention, and educational programs.

Are these reforms likely to reduce sexual victimization on college campuses? Evaluations of the first initiative point to encouraging effects of programs designed to improve self-defense tactics and assertiveness against potential perpetrators (for a review, Daigle, Fisher, & Stewart, 2009). Illustrative of this observation is a landmark 2005 study conducted by Brecklin and Ullman who examined a large sample (N = 1,623) of women attending 32 institutions in the U.S. In particular, the researchers sought to evaluate whether any differences existed between women who had completed defensive training compared to those who did not. Their results showed that among the students who reported experiencing a sexual attack, women with pre-assault training were more likely to say that their resistance stopped the offender or made the offender less aggressive than victims without training. The study also revealed that consistent with self-defense training hypotheses, women with training prior to their assaults were angrier and significantly less scared during the incident than women without training. There is additional evidence that rape aggression defense training received while attending college also improves outcomes among survivors of prior sexual assault, improving their levels of self-efficacy and confidence in engaging in risk avoidance behavior in the future (Pinciotti & Orcutt, 2018). Collectively, the findings from a larger body of research suggest the benefits of programs designed to empower college students against sexual victimization.

The implementation of bystander programs is also a recent initiative that has gained steam across campuses. As reviewed in our previous discussions, such programs are designed to encourage third parties to intervene (i.e., act as "capable bystanders") in situations that may progress to sexual assault (e.g., unconscious victim). Although premised logically, do these programs work to reduce sexual victimization? Early research conducted by Banyard and her colleagues (2007) suggests their utility in possibly preventing sexual victimization. In particular, Banyard, Moynihan, and Plante (2007) used an experimental design to assess the impact of a bystander initiative (e.g., based on a community responsibility model that teaches individuals how to intervene in high-risk situations) among college students. Specifically, 389 students were randomly assigned to a control group (no bystander education) or two experimental groups (one session of programming or three sessions of programming). In support of the bystander intervention logic, compared to those in the control condition, students in the two treatment groups were significantly more likely to exhibit improvements across a range of measures. That is, significant increases in prosocial bystander attitudes (e.g., "How likely are you to investigate if you are

© Aleutie/Shutterstock.com

awakened at night by someone calling for help?"), increased bystander efficacy ("How confident are you that you could ask a stranger who looks very upset at a party if they are ok or need help?"), and increases in self-reported bystander behaviors (e.g., "Have you walked a friend home from a party who has had too much to drink?") were observed. Additionally, Banyard et al. (2007) found evidence of a dose effect. Increases in bystander efficacy were greatest for students who participated in the three-session intervention. Notably, these effects lasted over a substantial period, at 4 and 12-month follow-ups. These patterns of improvement benefited both male and female students.

A later follow-up meta-analysis (study of all the studies in a particular area) which synthesized the results of 15 prior investigations revealed similarly positive benefits of bystander intervention (Kettrey & Marx, 2019). In particular, college students who completed bystander intervention training compared to students who did not showed stronger intentions to intervene in risky situations and a greater understanding of bystander intervention practices. Most beneficial was the finding that participants of bystander intervention training were significantly more likely to report actually intervening in prior situations. The meta-analysis was important for establishing that training had its most desirable impact on incoming and second-year students, compared to upper-class students. Having said that, bystander intervention effects depend on the quality of the intervention. Those that are brief, "one-shot" initiatives or are poorly conceptualized are not likely to be as effective as comprehensive initiatives. Additionally, despite the high rates of sexual violence experienced by sexual and gender minorities (SGM), few interventions have been developed to target SGM students (Kirk-Provencher, Spillane, Schick, Chalmers, Hawes, & Orchowski, 2021). For this reason, greater attention is needed toward creating bystander awareness programs tailored to serve diverse student populations.

A multi-faceted strategy is needed to effectively address campus sexual assault (Hirsch & Khan, 2020). To be clear, bystander intervention is just one tool that may contribute toward fulfilling that goal. Still, bystander awareness trainings—particularly those interventions that are administered to incoming students, well-designed, and inclusive—may be especially influential in ensuring greater capable guardianship thereby reducing the incidence of sexual assault and victimization on campus.

© CG_dmitriy/Shutterstock.com

© retrorocket/Shutterstock.com

Reflection **6**

Capable Bystander

Have you ever acted as a capable bystander (i.e., sought to remove a victim out of harm's way) in the past? If so, what was the context? Would you ever consider intervening in a potentially dangerous situation in the future? If so, what factors would motivate you to do so? If not, what concerns would you have?

More broadly, programs to educate students about sexual victimization have become typical nationally (Mancini & Budd, 2020). Do these efforts reduce the incidence of sexual assault on college campuses? The short answer is "potentially," but with important caveats. Students who completed a curriculum focused on teaching them verbal and physical resistance in risky situations had a reduced incidence of attempted rape (i.e., penetrative sex offense) and completed rape, and other forms of victimization (e.g., nonconsensual touching) one year later (Senn, Eliasziw, Barata, Thurston, Newby-Clark, Radtke, & Hobden, 2015). Moreover, interventions targeting male students seem particularly beneficial. One meta-analysis (study of a large body of research) found that male college students who complete sexual assault awareness programs are significantly less likely to report future perpetration of sexual assault (Wright, Zounlome, & Whiston, 2020).

However, it is equally true that some treatment modalities have less of an impact on outcomes. For example, in a large review of 69 studies, Anderson and Whiston (2005) found that length of programming, the content of the program, targeted group, and presenter characteristics predicted the impact of education. In particular, structured programming that is longer in duration (as opposed to vague, "one-shot" interventions) and facilitated by professionals (as opposed to peers or graduate students) had the most positive impact on increasing awareness of sexual assault and reducing attitudes conducive to the perpetration of sexual assault. Additionally, the influence of programming is most beneficial when it is targeted toward certain subcultures of students ("Greek" Life) and students of the same-sex. In comparison, other forms of programming were less impactful in changing attitudes and intentions (DeGue, 2014).

Later work suggests that prevention efforts that reflect a more intentional and proactive approach might be worthwhile to pursue. For example, education received *prior* to college enrollment might be especially beneficial in reducing sex crime risk. Undergraduates who reported being exposed to a K-12 school-based sex education program that promoted "refusal skills" (e.g., how to "say no" to unwanted sexual contact) were significantly less likely to experience sexual victimization in college. In contrast, "abstinence-only" instruction had no effect on subsequent sexual assault risk (Santelli et al., 2018).

In their 2020 landmark study of sexual assault at Columbia University, distinguished researchers Jennifer Hirsch and Shamus Khan analyzed five years' worth of data from the Sexual Health Initiative to Foster Transformation (SHIFT) project, which sought to understand the structural factors that contribute to campus sexual assault. Specifically, findings from a large quantitative survey as well as qualitative interviews, observations, and focus groups were analyzed and reported in their text, *Sexual Citizens*. From this analysis, Hirsch and Khan (2020) observed that many existing campus sex assault prevention efforts have traditionally focused on the individual perpetrator rather than the broader context in which victimization occurs. For this reason, they recommend reimagining sex education. For example, most students report that the quality of sexual education they received during high school was poor. Teachers delivering the material were usually "mortified" at having to teach it (Hirsch & Khan, 2020, p. xvii). Indeed, as Hirsch and Khan recount much of the content of traditional sexual education programs emphasize the negative aspects of unprotected sex such as unintended pregnancies and the transmission of sexually transmitted diseases (STDs). Accordingly, more effective education should start early (i.e., prior to college), and incorporate key concepts of "sexual citizenship," or the notion that all people are deserving of autonomy in navigating their sexual relationships. Comprehensive sexual education would also emphasize the more positive aspects of sexual encounters, or communicating what one wants out of the interaction (what Hirsch and Khan term "sexual projects"). Importantly, to be effective,

Hirsch and Khan (2020) advise that such training should also be inclusive, incorporating topics and situations relevant to LGBTQ students.

One final point bears mention. As summarized earlier, sexual consent laws vary by state. This point is important to emphasize when the focus is on crime prevention, and more generally, educational efforts, because acts that would be perfectly legal in one state, could be classified as a crime in another. Given the variation across states, students are encouraged to consult with their respective institution so they are informed about the policies and laws in their jurisdiction prior to engaging in sexual activity with others. Want to test your recall of what we covered in Chapter 3? Peruse the Chapter 3 Exercise on the following page. Our next unit, Chapter 4 is entitled "Social Activism, Unrest, and the College Campus." Given current discussions and debates about free speech, inequities, and higher education—particularly in the aftermath of the COVID-19 pandemic and murder of George Floyd—this is an especially "hot topic" on the typical college campus.

Theory and Practice

In Chapter 3, we covered three theoretical perspectives related to campus crime and then research-supported reforms for preventing crime. For this exercise, first articulate the logic and key determinant of crime behind each theory. Place your answers under question 1 ("Theory Summary"). Next, perform a web search of your university's website (the police department website may be a starting point) to determine if your university has implemented any of the programs we have reviewed. Record your answers under "Inventory of Policies at Your University." You will want to check off whether your institution has developed the practice and also note your source or link to the website.

1. Theory Summary

Theory	Logic?	Key Determinant of Crime?
Routine Activities		
Lifestyle		
Victim Precipitation		

2. Inventory of Policies at Your University

Practice	Institution Has? (✓)	Source/Link?
Blue Lights		
Crime Prevention App		
Safety Escort		
Substance Abuse Education		
Cyber-Related Education		
Self-Defense Courses		
Bystander Awareness Programs		
Sexual Victimization Education		

Social Activism, Unrest, and the College Campus

4

ACTIVATE YOUR THINKING

1. How have college students engaged in social activism in the past?

2. Why are universities typically places where social issues are debated and discussed?

3. What contemporary topics have become the subject of student protests and what has been the outcome of such activism?

4. What steps can be taken to ensure students are able to exercise their First Amendment right while maintaining campus safety?

LEARNING GOALS

- To contextualize current events from a historical lens
- To demonstrate awareness of the connection between college campuses and social activism
- To identify factors related to the unintended effects of protests and social activism
- To articulate how institutions can avoid the potential for demonstrations to "go wrong"
- To recount ways to protest peacefully, legally, and effectively

Chapter 4 focuses on a "special" or contemporary topic as of late, that of ensuring public safety during a time of social activism. The recent social unrest of 2020, stemming from the murder of George Floyd and other racialized injustices led to unprecedented protests and support for the Black Lives Matter (BLM) movement. However, such social activism undertaken by college students is not new. Historically, the college campus has been viewed as a place where there should be a free exchange of thought and where diverse views can be expressed (Van Dyke, 1998). This chapter unfolds in five parts. The first section summarizes the historical evolution of social activism on campus. The second section describes the events of 2020 and their impact on student protests. The third section illustrates "worst-case" scenarios when "demonstrations go wrong." The fourth section explores how public

Photo taken by Christina Mancini at the North Carolina Museum of History.

safety can be realized while institutions uphold the First Amendment rights of students and the university community. The last section offers suggestions for students who want to pursue activism safely and effectively.

History of Campus Social Activism

One of the first college protests in the U.S. can be traced to Harvard University nearly three hundred years ago. As retold by historians, in 1766, students at the esteemed college assembled to demand fresher food, most notably, higher quality butter in their dining halls (Lee, 2019).

In the 1960s and 1970s, American college students directed their social activism toward weightier issues. For instance, according to legal scholars, the advancement of the Civil Rights Movement—while the collective accomplishment of several integral groups of social reformers (Schmidt, 2018)—was partly realized through the actions of college students, particularly students identifying as Black and African American (Clayton, 2018). During the height of social activism in the 1960s, students organized voter-registration drives, led and participated in protests, and took part in sit-ins. According to a 1968 survey, one in five student protests that occurred in the 1960s featured the issue of civil rights (Anderson, 2015). Students were also active in protesting against the conflict in Vietnam, calling for the U.S. to withdraw its military presence (Small, 2002).

In contemporary eras, student activism has centered on similar themes of conflict and inequality. For instance, in the early 2000s, college students across the country demonstrated against the Iraq War and professors excused students who wished to protest against the conflict (Loviglio, 2003). Shortly after the hashtag #MeToo went viral on Twitter in 2017, college students took to the streets to advance the movement and demand fairer treatment of sex crime victims and survivors (Hartocollis, 2019).

Contemporary Student Activism Post-2020

Most recently, the murder of George Floyd on May 25, 2020 has mobilized students and the larger community to support actions condemning police brutality and the unfair treatment of African American/Black citizens by the criminal justice system. For example, one national survey of Americans conducted a month after Floyd's murder (Thomas & Menasce Horowitz, 2020) found 67 percent supported the Black Lives Matter (BLM, 2021) movement, "whose mission is to eradicate White supremacy and build local power to intervene in violence inflicted on Black communities by the state and vigilantes." Among students, approval of the movement is higher, with 8 out of 10 students expressing support of BLM (College Pulse, 2020).

Along with other BLM advocates, students have pushed for a variety of changes relevant not just for the legal system, but also applicable to post-secondary institutions. These changes include alternatives to campus policing, greater acknowledgement of student adversity, particularly for non-White students, hiring and retention of African American and Black faculty, and other remedies aligned with promoting diversity, equity, and inclusion (Dennon, 2020).

According to scholars, the pandemic has challenged students to reimagine their activism. With campuses closed during the height of BLM protests many students turned to social media to exercise their First Amendment privileges. Some have participated in virtual events, made donations to support social causes, and/or posted sentiments in favor of BLM and efforts to ensure racial equity and inclusion (Ezarik, 2021). Moreover, according to some accounts, the pandemic did not deter all students from protesting in traditional fashion. One in five college students reported participating in an in-person protest during the summer of 2020 (Ezarik, 2021)

Students are especially effective at spurring social change through their activism (Schmidt, 2018). First, they are particularly adept at mobilizing collective action toward important social issues. Second, college students often have greater social capital and resources than other groups, and thus may be more successful in promoting ideals and policies that would benefit marginalized and underserved populations (Wheatle, 2020). Having said that, some advocates who seek to promote greater student activism worry that with the advent of social media, students will turn to "slacktivism." Scholars have defined this behavior as "low-cost, low-risk participation in a protest effort," typically limited to the virtual world (e.g., social media, online communication; Smith, Krishna, & Al-Sinan, 2019, p. 183). Slacktivism can include hitting "like" to indicate one's support or approval for particular ideas or events on social media, signing online petitions advancing a cause for change, forwarding e-mails about social issues to others, or changing one's profile picture on a Facebook account, for example, to indicate solidarity with a particular social movement. Thus, the concern is that such acts are not as influential as "boots on the ground" activism (e.g., physically protesting in a public setting, donating to a cause, writing or meeting with a policymaker or legislator). As a counter-argument to this perspective, others see value in slacktivism and social media use in general. For example, some observers claim that such forms of relatively low-cost, low-risk activism could encourage greater social change by mobilizing groups whom might otherwise not unite to advance a social cause, and can, under certain conditions progress into actionable and more traditional forms of protest (e.g., Oh & Sundar, 2016).

Regardless of the form of activism, it is clear that college students' collective action can inspire change, particularly when it involves issues of higher education and topics affecting youthful populations. The question then becomes, what is needed to ensure the university community is tolerant of social activism and how can public safety be maintained? Before turning to that important question, the chapter first summarizes how demonstrations can go terribly wrong.

When Demonstrations Go Wrong

While the majority of campus protests that occur nationally are peaceful, some live in infamy. For example, in 1970, the Ohio National Guard shot several Kent State University demonstrators protesting against the Vietnam War, killing four and wounding several other students. According to a historical analysis, the shootings have "come to symbolize the deep political and social divisions that so sharply divided the country during the Vietnam War era" (Lewis & Hensley, 2021).

More recently, Americans were horrified by the loss of life and acts of violence committed at the "Unite the Right" rally, which occurred in July 2017 in the college town of Charlottesville, Virginia, home to the University of Virginia (UVA). Organizers of the Unite the Right rally sought to encourage a variety of "alt-right" groups to assemble to protest the city's removal of Confederate statutes, a move seen as an affront to "White civil rights" by adherents of the alt-right movement (Heapy, 2017, p. 23). The rally attracted counter-protestors, many of them UVA students. Overall, the rally resulted in one death, several injuries, arrests, and social unrest in the city and across the country. Many entities—the local government, the federal government, and to some extent, UVA—were criticized for a lack of preparation (Heaphy, 2017).

Social Activism, Sensitive Topics, and the Institution

Fortunately, incidents like the Kent State mass shooting and the Charlottesville tragedy are rare. Most demonstrations that occur on college campuses (or close by) are peaceful. College administrators have the difficult task of designing a campus that encourages student and community activism while also ensuring it is a safe space for all to assemble and exercise their right to free speech. This section reviews some trends in this direction.

In response to concerns about hate speech and its impact on marginalized groups, some institutions have designed "safe spaces" and encouraged the use of "trigger warnings" by faculty teaching sensitive topics. The first concept of safe spaces (or zones) refers more to an ideology than specific practice. As Ali (2017, p. 3) explains such practices "have ultimately centered on increasing the safety and visibility of marginalized or oppressed community members." Thus, safe spaces could encompass physical areas (e.g., a center for underserved students) or virtual places (e.g., an online support group for minority students). In contrast, trigger warnings refer to an advisory that a course or classroom discussion may delve into difficult or upsetting content (e.g., sexual assault). While many colleges and universities have implemented some form of these practices over the last decade, there has been increased criticism and legal scrutiny surrounding the restrictions and the general approach to regulate speech on college campuses. In 2016, the Dean of Students at the University of Chicago (John "Jay" Ellison), sent a letter to new students emphasizing that due to the premium placed on academic freedom and the free exchange of ideas, the University "does not condone the creation of intellectual 'safe spaces,' where individuals can retreat from ideas and perspectives at odds with their own" (Ellison, 2020). There is the additional concern that institutional-level attempts to restrict speech, even if it is well intentioned (e.g., to protect marginalized students) may not hold up to Constitutional challenges. For example, a recent incident at Salisbury State University in Maryland highlights this point (Anderson, 2020). As an *Inside Higher Ed* article recounted the president of the university, Charles Wight, in responding to an incident in which a student used racist language in a text message to another, explained how options to punish the student were limited:

> "I want to be honest with you . . . as a public university, the law requires that we must respect free speech, no matter how much we abhor what is said or what is written. It would be illegal for us to take punitive action against anyone simply for their words, no matter how vile or hateful they might be."

Instead, President Wight recommended students protest against offensive rhetoric. Simply put, "the First Amendment allows lots of breathing room for the messy, chaotic, ad hominem, passionate, and even bigoted speech that is part and parcel of American politics" (Lindsay, 2020).

To promote a more informed and civil conversation about difficult topics, some institutions have encouraged students and faculty to complete diversity and inclusion education and training programs. This emphasis is particularly important for conversations surrounding sensitive concepts, like race, class, and gender (Khalid & Snyder, 2021). Such trainings usually involve workshops, small group breakouts, and simulations to inspire candid conversations among participants (Khalid & Snyder, 2021). At some colleges, students must complete (or are encouraged to complete) diversity and inclusion training (Kolodner, 2020).

Some observers have argued however that such programs are not enough to promote inclusive dialogue and that institutions should focus on other initiatives, such as the hiring (and retention) of non-White faculty, particularly at the tenure-track level (National Center for Education Statistics, 2020b). The tenure-track distinction is an important one in higher education. Typically, due to the stronger assurance of academic freedom that tenure brings with it, tenured faculty are in positions to shape policies, initiatives, and programs more so than adjunct or non-tenured professors. In some colleges, a student can complete an entire degree without taking a course taught by an African American/Black professor (Kolodner, 2020). Students from minority backgrounds, particularly, African American/Black and Latino/Latinx students, are entering college at higher rates than ever before (Association of American Colleges and Universities, 2019) meaning many students will earn their college degrees without ever having the opportunity to engage with professors who have similar racial and ethnic backgrounds. Research suggests that exposure to non-White teachers and mentors imparts profound benefits to students, particularly for Black males, improving their academic performance and professional ambitions (Figlio, 2017; Moore & Toliver, 2010). While many colleges and universities seem to acknowledge the dearth of minority faculty and have committed to addressing it (Kolodner, 2020), the current reality is that Black/African American and Latino/Latinx instructors are underrepresented at all levels, including as tenured faculty (National Center for Education Statistics, 2020b).

To summarize, college administrators have the unenviable task of crafting policies and procedures that do not unduly restrict free speech while also ensuring the safety and inclusion of all members of the university community. While difficult, it is an essential exercise given that "student activism is essentially the embodiment of what higher education seeks to do, which is cultivate and actively engage those concerned about issues that matter" (Rogers, 2018).

Social Activism and Sensitive Topics: Best Practices for Students

At some point in your college career, it is likely you will feel passionately about a social issue or problem, be it of local or national importance. Thus, you may find yourself in a position of wanting to express your perspective. As we have already reviewed, activism occurs across many forms. For this reason, the below bullet points are rough guidelines concerning how to safely, civilly, and effectively communicate your view. Your voice matters!

1. First, identify how you can become involved. Recognize that there are many forms of activism. Choose the type of activism that works best for you (e.g., joining a march, donating to a cause, volunteering, starting a new student organization, participating in a virtual event).
2. Second, understand the law. Be aware of the behaviors that are acceptable and those that are not. This will depend on the type of activism in which you engage, the state in which you live, and the institution of which you attend. Private colleges and universities are permitted greater latitude in restricting free speech than public ones (Kaplin & Lee, 2014). Regardless of the institution, consider having a legal advocate on standby or ask a trusted mentor for advice.
3. Third, when protesting, play it safe! Keep your message peaceful and avoid groups or individuals who are aggressive or becoming violent. The First Amendment does not protect one from prosecution for making threats of harm to others or for acts of civil disobedience (e.g., not following law enforcement's orders). This is true in the virtual sense, too. Remember, social media posts last forever.
4. On that note, if you see something, say something! Consider using an app (e.g., LiveSafe, or specific one for your college) to report any criminal behavior.
5. Reflect on your experience. Share your experience in the classroom and consider networking with similarly minded groups.

Snapshot Summary Box 7 compares and contrasts the different types of activism and provides links to resources to help you prepare for your own activism. The Chapter 4 Exercise tests your comprehension of key concepts and objectives. The text concludes with a review of important "take-aways" for understanding campus crime and efforts to prevent it (Chapter 5).

Snapshot Summary

7 | **Types of Activism and Resources for Effective Participation**

Type of Activism	Examples	Link for Resource
Online	"Like" a post; retweet/advertise post on personal social media account; participate in online forums; sign an online petition	https://www.publicservi-cedegrees.org/resources/student-guide-to-online-activism/
Financial	Donate to an organization; contribute to campaigns of lawmakers/policy-makers who advocate change; start a "GoFundMe" or crowdsource page to advance a social issue	https://www.cnn.com/2020/06/19/us/how-to-donate-social-justice-funds-trnd/index.html
Physical	March in a protest; "walk-out" of a class or social event; take part in a demonstration on campus	https://www.wired.com/story/how-to-protest-safely-gear-tips/

Social Activism on Campus

Chapter 4 explored a "special topic"—that of student social activism. For this assignment, please respond to the questions related to this theme below.

1. Describe the history of social activism on campus in the U.S. Why do you think the college campus has become a key environment for protesting social issues?

2. Chapter 4 reviewed instances in which "demonstrations can go wrong." Discuss at least one of these cases. What actions can colleges take to reduce the occurrence of violence and unrest for future protests?

3. Identify and describe the types of social activism that exist. Which types of activism do you think would be most appealing to students and why?

Resources for Victims and Those Concerned about Crime

5

1. What is the Victims' Rights Movement?

2. What are the rights of students who are victimized?

3. What resources exist for victims of campus crime?

4. How can we understand the victim experience?

LEARNING GOALS

- To be familiar with the historical development of victim-centered laws and policies
- To demonstrate knowledge of the legal rights afforded to crime victims
- To identify resources for students who are criminally victimized
- To appreciate and acknowledge the victim experience in accountability efforts

Our final focus centers on victim treatment and resources for those concerned about victimization. This dimension is critical given concerns that the justice system typically takes into account the needs of those who perpetrate crimes at the expense of those who are harmed by crime. In what follows, "victims' rights" and the victim experience are explored. This discussion includes outlining the types of resources available to those harmed by crime, including campus crime. This sub-section concludes with a summary of what victims might expect should the perpetrator be identified and processed by the institution and/or the criminal justice system. The issues explored in this chapter have direct relevance to college students, and more generally, members of the campus community concerned with crime. Victims of crime have a variety of rights but many, in particular students, are likely not aware of these services and sources of support. For this reason, familiarity with these specific resources may in part help with facilitating victim recovery and assistance.

Victims' Rights

It is often said that the *criminal* justice system unfairly revolves around those who commit offenses and ignores the needs and suffering of the victim. This realization, in part, has prompted the "Victims' Rights Movement." David Garland (2001, p. 121), a prominent criminologist on the faculty of New York University noted that since the 1980s, "police, prosecution, and court agencies have increasingly made it their policy to ensure that victims are kept informed, treated with more sensitivity, offered access to support, and given compensation for their injuries." As this observation implies, victim services have been prioritized under this shift in the justice system. Broadly, these new rights and programs are two-pronged. In contrast to earlier decades, under the Victim's Rights Movement, victims now have the option to be involved in criminal court proceedings. Additionally, all states and the federal government have developed and implemented victim compensation or assistance programs. This movement and the new policies that flowed from it, are further discussed below.

Victims' Rights Movement. Under President Reagan, in 1984 the U.S. Congress enacted the Victims of Crime Act (VOCA). The Act accomplished two goals. Given concerns related to the absence of victim assistance, it established a victim compensation fund that provides victim services through fines and fees levied against those convicted of federal offenses. In addition, the law introduced federal legislation pertaining to victims' rights and services and assistance in the criminal justice system. Currently, the federal agency, the Office for Victims of Crime (OVC), distributes these resources and services to victims, provides training for victim advocates and states, and disseminates information about victimization to concerned citizens (OVC, 2020b).

Involvement in Court Process. With the emergence of the Victims' Rights Movement, victims are now entitled to a variety of rights during the justice process. While these rights vary by state, basic protections include: the right to give victim impact statements during sentencing, receive notifications about on-going court proceedings involving their case, to be notified about information regarding offender conviction, sentencing, imprisonment, and release, the option to request an order of restitution from the offender, the right to reasonable protection from the offender, and the right to be informed of these rights (Federal Bureau of Investigation, 2021b). Most states have also enacted laws to protect specific classes of victims such as victims of sexual offenses during criminal proceedings (Mancini, 2021). These reforms, known as "rape shield" laws have two goals. First, the legislation protects victims by barring the media from releasing identifying information. A second feature of the law is that it prevents the defense in criminal proceedings from "blaming the victim." With respect to this latter provision, the defendant cannot claim as a defense that the victim's attire or prior sexual history indicated consent.

To be clear, these general provisions related to court proceedings also extend to students attending a college or university who report the offense and wish to pursue criminal charges; having said that, schools typically go beyond these considerations. As reviewed earlier, to comply with federal reporting mandates, schools often assist victims with filing a police report (University of Nevada-Las Vegas, 2021). Universities may also have a victim advocate on staff who can walk the victim through the court process (University of Tampa, 2021).

Victim Assistance. Over the last two decades, most states and the federal government have recognized that criminal victimization is associated with numerous financial and health-related costs. For this reason, additional protections have been instituted such as developing programs that financially compensate victims for lost wages, medical and therapy bills, and other related costs incurred by the victimization. As explained earlier, the OVC, a federal agency funded by fees and fines paid by federal offenders, distributes federal victim compensation and assistance and also provides resources and technical training to jurisdictions concerning the development of victim programs (OVC, 2020a). Depending on the institution, student-victims may be eligible for other considerations. For instance,

© Monkey Business Images/Shutterstock.com

the SaVE Act stipulates that students who experience victimization be given the option of seeking academic accommodations such as extensions to course work and scheduling flexibility (Marshall, 2014). Universities with health care centers may also offer victims access to mental health services and counseling (Sabina, Verdiglione, & Zadnik, 2017).

Victims of Crime—What to Expect

As illustrated by the previous discussion, criminal victimization is a traumatic experience. At the same time, crime victims often have many obligations. Reporting the crime to police, working with the court system, and disclosing the victimization to family, friends, and employers are just a sampling of these post-offense experiences. The current discussion describes the typical victim experience after the crime. Attention is first given to the criminal court phase, and then turns to civil sanctions. Finally, given the focus on campus crime, we briefly touch on the university accountability system with a special emphasis on the victim perspective.

Criminal Court Proceedings. Before we turn to what victims can expect during the court process, it is imperative to separate fact from fiction. Popular shows like *Law & Order: Special Victims Unit* and *CSI* purportedly depict the inner-workings of the court system. In many of these dramatized depictions, "justice" is served (typically, in under an hour)—a perpetrator is identified and arrested, physical evidence is collected and analyzed, and a dramatic trial ensues.

Even so, many of these depictions of the criminal courts are not entirely accurate. For instance, trials very rarely occur. Over 90 percent of defendants plead guilty to some offense (Siegel & Worrall, 2018). Additionally, although court proceedings in these fictionalized accounts wrap up in around 60 minutes (less commercials of course), in the real world, criminal cases—even those disposed of through plea bargaining—can drag on for months and even years.

What do these observations mean for crime victims? The simple answer is that victims seeking justice in the courts often have a long and sometimes frustrating journey ahead of them. Here is a

© felipe caparros/Shutterstock.com

rough sketch of what student-victims can expect as they progress through the criminal justice system. Victims who report the crimes committed against them will first have interaction with police. During the investigatory phase, law enforcement officers will typically ask the victim several questions regarding the offense. Depending on the nature of the crime, victims may be asked to undergo a medical evaluation to collect forensic or physical evidence. Officers may request that victims participate in a line-up or work with a sketch artist to develop a composite picture of the perpetrator.

If law enforcement has identified a suspect and determines that sufficient evidence exists for an arrest, the case will move toward the prosecution stage. Here again, victims will work closely with the government. The decision to prosecute, referred to as prosecutorial discretion, means that prosecutors ultimately decide which charges are dismissed and which go forward (Stewart, 1987). Typically, victims are the state's best witnesses, particularly for crimes in which there is an absence of forensic evidence or eyewitness accounts. Thus, victims will work closely with these court actors. If criminal charges go forward, the odds are great that defendants will plead guilty to at least some offense rather than go to trial (Siegel & Worrall, 2018). There are various types of plea bargains. For example, defendants may accept a deal in which they admit guilt to a lesser offense than the initial charge. Alternatively, other plea negotiations can occur in which some charges are dropped in exchange for convictions on others. The plea bargaining process is important to emphasize because depending on the specific state statute, victims may have the opportunity to voice input into possible sanctions and punishments (O'Hear, 2007).

What might victims expect if defendants choose to assert their 6th Amendment privilege to a jury trial? In this rare instance, victims will likely have to testify regarding the crime committed against them. Witnesses in jury proceedings face direct examination by the prosecutor. Generally, since the state is seeking a conviction against the accused, this process is less stressful for victims than cross examination. In this latter stage, the defense questions the witness about the crime. This proceeding may be more traumatic for the victim than direct examination because the defense can imply that the victim is not credible, has a poor memory, or in some way is responsible for the offense. In recent years, as described earlier, the criminal courts have

© Junial Enterprises/Shutterstock.com

limited "victim blaming" defenses in instances of alleged sexual assault. Even so, there are exceptions. For instance, appellate courts have ruled that the accused can ask about the victim's prior sexual history (e.g., a prior sexual relationship with the defendant) *if* it is directly related to contact with the defendant (Anderson, 2004); judges, though, are responsible for weighing the rights of the accused (e.g., right to assert a defense to the criminal charges) with those of crime victims (Mancini, 2021).

According to federal statistics, two out of three felony defendants who go to trial are ultimately found guilty of a crime by a jury of their peers (Cohen & Kyckelhahn, 2010; Durose, Farole, & Rosenmerkel, 2009). Put differently, the odds are in favor of the state that the accused will face some type of punishment. Victims may still participate in the court process even after a criminal conviction. For instance, during the sentencing phase, which follows the guilt/innocence phase, victims typically have the option to submit a victim impact statement (Erez & Rogers, 1999; Kunst, de Groot, Meester, & van Doorn, 2021) or testimony to the court regarding how the crime has affected the victim's quality of life, relationships, health, and other aspects. In dispositions resulting in a prison sentence, most states promise to notify victims regarding where offenders will be incarcerated. States that practice parole may also permit victims to testify at parole board hearings. Additionally, some states bar offenders who are reentering society from living in close proximity to their prior victims (Mancini, 2021).

Civil Sanctions. Civil court is a second option for victims who are unsatisfied with criminal proceedings, or feel entitled to monetary or financial compensation stemming from their injury. Notably, criminal and civil proceedings are generally mutually exclusive—meaning a victim can seek civil judgments even in cases where the offender has been convicted of the crime against them. Indeed, plaintiffs (in this case, victims) can submit the defendants' prior criminal convictions as evidence in civil proceedings. There is one exception, however. Nolo contendere ("no contest") pleas prevent the admission as evidence, the defendant's guilty plea, since technically, under this system, the defendant does not accept or deny responsibility for the charges but rather agrees to accept the court's punishment (Bibas, 2003). These types of bargains are rarely used in felony cases. Rather, they apply almost exclusively to misdemeanor offenses (del Carmen, 2013). For the plea to be granted, the approval of the prosecution or court is typically needed.

To a large extent, civil courts differ from criminal courts. The punishment resulting from a civil sanction is not prison or jail, but rather a civil or monetary judgement in favor of one party (National Center for Victims of Crime, 2015). Additionally, in a criminal case, the state or federal government brings charges against a defendant. In civil proceedings, this does not occur. Rather, victims (plaintiffs in the civil court system) would need to initiate civil proceedings against the accused (or the defendant). The standard of proof of culpability that one party (the plaintiff or victim) would need to demonstrate in civil court—"preponderance of evidence"—is much less than the "beyond a reasonable doubt" standard in the criminal court system. There are other differences that are notable for victims. For instance, many victim protection statutes, such as rape shield laws and victim impact statement opportunities, generally do not apply to civil court proceedings (Hines, 2011). Additionally, victims do not typically have access to victim advocacy services and support that may be available in the criminal courts. Not least, as discussed earlier, in the civil system justice is not served through a prison or jail sanction, but rather through a monetary judgement. For victims, this latter outcome may feel significantly less satisfying than criminal punishment. Moreover, although civil judgements are binding legal orders, there are no guarantees that crime victims will receive compensation from defendants, particularly if they are impoverished or currently incarcerated.

Disciplinary Review Boards. One final level of accountability occurs at the institutional level. As we explored earlier, in instances of student against student victimization (and student-faculty victimization), student-victims can seek punishment at their respective college or university against the person who may have harmed them. How is this possible? The simple answer is that institutions typically outline what behavior constitutes a violation of the university honor code. Thus, harming other students—physically, or sexually, for instance, would fall under these guidelines. Put differently, this system allows the institution to hold students accountable for violations of the student conduct code.

The university accountability process is clearly distinct from the civil and criminal court options. Perhaps most obvious, universities and colleges do not have the legal authority to incarcerate or otherwise detain students who have violated the honor code. Indeed, the most severe sanction is expulsion. Moreover, unlike the state in criminal court proceedings, the university does not bring charges against suspected perpetrators. Rather, both parties present their case and the judicial board determines whether enough evidence exists to suggest a violation of the student honor code. As reviewed earlier, but relevant here again, the standard of evidence applied in judicial board hearings has varied. Typically, the "preponderance of evidence" standard is used across many institutions (Karjane et al., 2002). It is a markedly lower bar than the criminal court standard of "beyond a reasonable doubt." The terminology used in the judicial review board system is also distinct (Karjane et al., 2002); in this latter system, victims are referred to as "complainants" or "accusers" and (alleged) perpetrators as "respondents" or the "accused," rather than the prototypical criminal justice labels of "victims" and "defendants." In reference to evidence, here again, review boards are limited in comparison to the justice system. In contrast to law enforcement agencies, universities and colleges do not have the authority to issue subpoenas that compel witness testimony nor search warrants to seize personal property and incriminating evidence.

How is culpability assessed and what might the victim expect? Contrary to the criminal court system, jurors are not used in assessing perpetrator guilt. Instead, institutions appoint judicial board members. Although the composition varies across colleges, generally students, faculty, and staff volunteer to hear and decide on cases (Karjane et al., 2002). While guidance concerning specific grievance procedures has varied across different presidential administrations, typically, federal law requires that post-secondary institutions provide both "complainants" (victims) and "respondents" (the accused) similar rights. These procedural safeguards include the right to an adviser, the right to receive notice of decisions at the same time, the right to appeal the decision, and other provisions (Mancini, 2021).

Snapshot Summary Box 8 compares and contrasts the three forms of accountability—criminal proceedings, civil court sanctioning, and disciplinary review board process—that we have just discussed. The Chapter 5 Exercise tests your comprehension of key concepts and objectives. The text concludes with a review of important "take-aways" for understanding campus crime and efforts to prevent it.

Serving Crime Victims

Now that you are aware of the many programs designed to assist crime victims, would you ever consider working in a field that serves crime victims? Why or why not?

8

Snapshot Summary

Three Forms of Accountability, by Feature

Type of Accountability	Level	Adjudicating Body	Ultimate Outcome	Proceedings
Criminal Courts	Government	Jury of peers	Death; prison sentence	Trials; plea bargaining negotiations
Civil Courts	Individuals	Jury of peers	Monetary settlement; fines	Trials; settlement negotiations
Disciplinary Review Boards	University	Judicial hearing officers	Expulsion	Judicial hearings

The Victim Experience

This exercise tests your recall concerning our earlier discussions about Victims' Rights and the victim experience. Given this emphasis, you will first want to describe the victims' rights movement and its significance. Turning to our other focus, in the "Accountability, by Type," table, provide a short description and outline some the limitations for each practice.

1. How would you describe "victims' rights?" What is the historical significance of the Victims' Rights Movement in the U.S.? What rights can crime victims expect in the justice system and beyond?

2. Accountability, by Type

Accountability System	Brief Description	Limitations
Criminal Courts		
Civil Courts		
Disciplinary Review Boards		

Concluding Remarks

In many ways, criminologists bear the burden of delivering bad news! In contrast to other fields, we study behavior and phenomena that are fear-inducing and in some instances, make people feel uncomfortable. Perhaps this is why we would like to ignore the crime problem on occasion or think that victimization happens to "other people." However, with that tendency comes consequences.

Many individuals who experience crime, even serious acts of violence, can go on to lead fulfilling and happy lives. The simple reality is that in some cases crimes occur that are senseless and random. Having said that, we can all practice steps to reduce our chances of experiencing victimization. To be sure, crime is not a light-hearted topic to cover, but it is imperative that students, many of whom are "on their own" for the first time in their lives, understand this very real threat to their safety and livelihoods. Below are my five top "take-aways" concerning this text that have the most practical relevance to your daily life. The bolded portions refer to specific actions you can take now to protect yourself during your college career.

1. First, campuses *are* relatively safe places! Having said that, college students may be at risk of experiencing certain offenses related to their lifestyle or perceived vulnerability. **Reduce your risk—check out the Clery Act reports on your campus**: http://ope.ed.gov/security/

2. Second, estimating the extent of the crime problem on campus is a complicated feat. **Be prepared, not scared! Becoming a crime savvy person will allow you to draw your own conclusions about the nature and extent of campus crime. Stay up-to-date with the latest federal data about criminal victimization across universities**: https://ope.ed.gov/campussafety/#/

3. Institutions of higher learning have invested much time and monetary resources in crime prevention. **Don't let those dollars go to waste! Take advantage of these programs and policies.** Check out your school's police department or campus security website for specific information. Encourage your school to use tools designed to enhance crime reporting, like the Live Safe App: http://www.livesafemobile.com/

4. Many factors may affect offending and predict victimization. Research-supported strategies are most effective in ensuring public safety. **Do you! Gauge your individual victimization risk by assessing your personal characteristics and lifestyle factors. Prevent crime by implementing self-protective measures into practice.**

5. The gains of the Victims' Rights movement, prominent in the 1980s, extend to victims of campus crimes. As a student, you are entitled to these safeguards. **Know your rights and exercise them!** If you are the victim or survivor of a crime and feel you are not being treated fairly, contact the U.S. Department of Education and submit a complaint via the Clery Act Compliance Division at: clery@ed.gov. You can also call 1-800-4-FED-AID (1-800-433-3243).

References

Abramson, P. (2004). Special report: College housing 2004. *College Planning & Management, 6*, 22–42.

Aisenberg, S. (2011, May 27). Is your campus doing enough to keep you safe? *USA Today*. http://college.usatoday.com/2011/05/27/is-your-campus-doing-enough-to-keep-you-safe/

Ali, D. (2017). *Safe spaces and brave spaces: Historical context and recommendations for student affairs professionals*. Washington, D.C.: NASPA Student Affairs Administrators in Higher Education.

Allan, E. J., Kerschner, D., & Payne, J. M. (2019). College student hazing experiences, attitudes, and perceptions: Implications for prevention. *Journal of Student Affairs Research and Practice, 56*, 32–48.

Anderson, G. (2020). When free speech and racist speech collide. *Inside Higher Ed*. https://www.insidehighered.com/news/2020/06/23/first-amendment-response-first-response-racism-campus

Anderson, M. (2002). From chastity requirement to sexuality license: Sexual consent and a new rape shield law. *George Washington Law Review, 70*, 51–165.

Anderson, M. D. (2015). The other student activists. *The Atlantic*. https://www.theatlantic.com/education/archive/2015/11/student-activism-history-injustice/417129/

Anderson, N. (2014, December 15). Colleges often reluctant to expel for sexual violence—with U-Va. a prime example. *Washington Post*. http://www.washingtonpost.com/local/education/colleges-often-reluctant-to-expel-for-sexual-violence--with-u-va-a-prime-example/2014/12/15/307c5648-7b4e-11e4-b821-503cc7efed9e_story.html

Anderson, R. E., Silver, K. E., Ciampaglia, A. M., Vitale, A. M., & Delahanty, D. L. (2021). The frequency of sexual perpetration in college men: A systematic review of reported prevalence rates from 2000 to 2017. *Trauma, Violence, & Abuse, 23*, 481–495.

Anderson, L. A., & Whiston, S. C. (2005). Sexual assault education programs: A meta-analytic examination of their effectiveness. *Psychology of Women Quarterly, 29*, 374–388.

Arria, A. M., Caldeira, K. M., Allen, H. K., Bugbee, B. A., Vincent, K. B., & O'Grady, K. E. (2017). Prevalence and incidence of drug use among college students: An 8-year longitudinal analysis. *American Journal of Drug and Alcohol Abuse, 43*, 711–718.

Association of American Colleges and Universities. (2019). *College students are more diverse than ever, faculty and administrators are not*. https://www.aacu.org/aacu-news/newsletter/2019/march/facts-figures

Bakeman, J. (2015). Sexual violence law specialist threatens SUNY over affirmative consent. *Politico*. https://www.politico.com/states/new-york/albany/story/2015/02/sexual-violence-law-specialist-threatens-suny-over-affirmative-consent-019969

Banyard, V. L., Moynihan, M. M., & Plante, E. G. (2007). Sexual violence prevention through bystander education: An experimental evaluation. *Journal of Community Psychology, 35*, 463–481.

Barr, L. (2018). For safety on campuses, law enforcement increasingly turns to apps. *ABC News*. https://abcnews.go.com/US/safety-campuses-law-enforcement-increasingly-turns-apps/story?id=57558628

Bauer-Wolf, J. (2020). The Ed Dept. is leaning on mediation to clear backlog of sexual violence cases, sources say. *Education Dive*. https://www.educationdive.com/news/the-ed-dept-is-leaning-on-mediation-to-clear-backlog-of-sexual-violence-cas/573582/

Baum, K., & Klaus, P. (2005). *Violent victimization of college students, 1995–2002.* Washington, D.C.: Bureau of Justice Statistics.

Bibas, S. (2003). Harmonizing substantive criminal law values and criminal procedure: The case of Alford and nolo contendere pleas. *Cornell Law Review, 88,* 1361–1411.

Binkley, C., Wagner, M., Riepenhoff, J., & Gregory, S. (2014, November 23). College disciplinary boards impose slight penalties for serious crimes. *Columbus Times Dispatch.* http://www.dispatch.com/content/stories/local/2014/11/23/campus-injustice.html

Black Lives Matter. (2021). *Black Lives Matter: About.* https://blacklivesmatter.com/about/

Branch Associates. (2002). *NetSmartz evaulation project: Internet safety training for children and youth ages 6 to 18.* Atlanta, GA: Boys and Girls Clubs of America and National Center for Missing and Exploited Children.

Broidy, L. M., Daday, J. K., Crandall, C. S., Sklar, D. P., & Jost, P. F. (2006). Exploring demographic, structural, and behavioral overlap among homicide offenders and victims. *Homicide Studies, 10,* 155–180.

Bromley, M. L. (1995). Factors associated with college crimes: Implications for campus police. *Journal of Police and Criminal Psychology, 10,* 13–19.

Bureau of Justice Statistics. (2021). *National Crime Victimization Survey (NCVS).* Washington, D.C.: Author.

Butler, L. C., Lee, H., & Fisher, B. S. (2019). Less safe in the ivory tower: Campus sexual assault policy in the Trump administration. *Victims & Offenders, 14,* 979–996.

Campbell, D. T., & Stanley, J. (1963). *Experimental and quasi-experimental designs for research.* Boston: Houghton-Mifflin.

Cantor, D., et al., Fisher, B., Chinball, S., Harps, S., Townsend, R., Thomas, G. . . . Madden, K. (2019). *Report on the AAU Campus Climate Survey on Sexual Assault and Sexual Misconduct: Revised.* Washington, D.C.: Association of American Universities.

Cantor, D., et al., Fisher, B., Chibnall, S., Townsend, R., Lee, H., Bruce, C. . . . Thomas, G. (2015). *Report on the AAU campus climate survey of sexual assault and sexual misconduct.* Washington, D.C.: Association of American Universities.

Carey, K. B., Scott-Sheldon, L. A., Carey, M. P., & DeMartini, K. S. (2007). Individual-level interventions to reduce college student drinking: A meta-analytic review. *Addictive Behaviors, 32,* 2469–2494.

Carey, K. B., Scott-Sheldon, L. A., Garey, L., Elliott, J. C., & Carey, M. P. (2016). Alcohol interventions for mandated college students: A meta-analytic review. *Journal of Consulting and Clinical Psychology, 84,* 619–632.

Centers for Disease Control. (2015). *Sexual violence: Prevention strategies.* Atlanta, GA: Author.

Chen, B., Seilhamer, R., Bennett, L., & Bauer, S. (2015). Students' mobile learning practices in higher education: A multi-year study. *Educause Review.* https://er.educause.edu/articles/2015/6/students-mobile-learning-practices-in-higher-education-a-multiyear-study

Chibnall, S., Wallace, M., Leicht, C., & Lunghofer, L. (2006). *I-SAFE evaluation: Final report.* Fairfax, VA: Caliber.

Clayton, D. M. (2018). Black lives matter and the civil rights movement: A comparative analysis of two social movements in the United States. *Journal of Black Studies, 49,* 448–480.

Clery Center. (2021). *Clery Act policy*. https://clerycenter.org/policy-resources/

Cohen, L. E., & Felson, M. (1979). Social change and crime rate trends: A routine activity approach. *American Sociological Review, 44,* 588–608.

Cohen, T. H., & Kyckelhahn, T. (2010). *Felony defendants in large urban counties, 2006.* Washington, D.C.: Bureau of Justice Statistics.

Coker, A. L., Bush, H. M., Fisher, B. S., Swan, S. C., Williams, C. M., Clear, E. R., & DeGue, S. (2016). Multi-college bystander intervention evaluation for violence prevention. *American Journal of Preventive Medicine, 50,* 295–302.

Coray, E. (2016). Victim protection or revictimization: Should college disciplinary boards handle sexual assault claims? *Boston College Journal of Law and Social Justice, 36,* 59–90.

College Pulse. (2020). 07/03/20: *Weekly Q's poll.* https://f.hubspotusercontent00.net/hubfs/5666503/070320-Weekly percent20Qs percent20Poll.pdf

Daigle, L. E., Fisher, B. S., & Stewart, M. (2009). The effectiveness of sexual victimization prevention among college students: A summary of "what works." *Victims and Offenders, 4,* 398–404.

Daigle, L. E., Johnston, T., Azimi, A., & Felix, S. N. (2019). Violent and sexual victimization among American and Canadian college students: Who is more at risk and are the risk factors invariant? *Journal of School Violence, 18,* 226–240.

Daly, M., & Wilson, M. (1988). *Homicide.* New York: Aldine de Gruyter.

Davis, T. L., & Liddell, D. L. (2002). Getting inside the house: The effectiveness of a rape prevention program for college fraternity men. *Journal of College Student Development, 43,* 35–50.

DeGue, S. (2015). *Preventing sexual violence on college campuses: Lessons from research and practice.* Atlanta: Centers for Disease Control.

DeKeseredy, W., Nolan, J. J., & Hall-Sanchez, A. (2019). Hate crimes and bias incidents in the ivory tower: Results from a large-scale campus survey. *American Behavioral Scientist.* https://doi.org/0002764219831733

del Carmen, R. (2013). *Criminal procedure: Law and practice* (9th ed.). Belmont, CA: Wadsworth/Cengage.

de León, K., & Jackson, H. B. (2015). Opinion: Why we made 'yes means yes' California law. *Washington Post.* https://www.washingtonpost.com/news/in-theory/wp/2015/10/13/why-we-made-yes-means-yes-california-law/

Dennon, A. (2020, June 7). Students demand racial justice and equity on campus. *Better Colleges.* https://www.bestcolleges.com/blog/college-student-activists-black-lives-matter/

Dobrin, A. (2001). The risk of offending on homicide victimization: A case control study. *Journal of Research in Crime and Delinquency, 38,* 154–173.

Durose, M., Farole, D., & Rosenmerkel, S. (2009). *Felony sentences in state courts, 2006.* Washington, D.C.: Bureau of Justice Statistics.

Drysdale, D. A., Modzeleski, W., & Simons, A. B. (2010). *Campus attacks: Targeted violence affecting institutions of higher education.* Washington, D.C.: Federal Bureau of Investigation.

Ellison, J. (2016). *Dear class of 2020 student.* https://news.uchicago.edu/sites/default/files/attachments/Dear_Class_of_2020_Students.pdf

Erez, E., & Rogers, L. (1999). Victim impact statements and sentencing outcomes and processes: The perspectives of legal professionals. *British Journal of Criminology, 39,* 216–239.

Ezarik, M. (2021). More discussion than action: Racial justice on campus. *Inside Higher Ed.* https://www.insidehighered.com/news/2021/05/06/what-students-think-about-racial-justice-efforts-campus

Family Educational Rights and Privacy Act. (1974). 20 U.S.C.A. Section 1232g. [Buckley Amendment.] (1991). *Implementing regulations* 34 C.F.R. 99.3. Fed. Reg. 56, Section 117, 28012.

Federal Bureau of Investigation. (2021a). *Uniform Crime Reports.* Washington, D.C.: Author.

Federal Bureau of Investigation. (2021b). *Rights of federal crime victims.* Washington, D.C.: Author.

Fernandez, A., & Lizotte, A. J. (1995). An analysis of the relationship between campus crime and community crime: Reciprocal effects? In B. S. Fisher & J. J. Sloan (Eds.), *Campus crime: Legal, social, and policy perspectives* (pp. 79–102). Springfield, IL: Charles C. Thomas.

Field, A. T. (2018). What happened after 2 colleges banned hard liquor at fraternities. *The Chronicle of Higher Education.* https://www.chronicle.com/article/what-happened-after-2-colleges-banned-hard-liquor-at-fraternities/

Figlio, D. (2017). The importance of a diverse teaching force. *Brookings Institute.* https://www.brookings.edu/research/the-importance-of-a-diverse-teaching-force/

Finkelhor, D., Walsh, K., Jones, L., Mitchell, K., & Collier, A. (2020). Youth internet safety education: Aligning programs with the evidence base. *Trauma, Violence, & Abuse.* https://doi.org/10.1177/1524838020916257

Finn, J. (2004). A survey of online harassment at a university campus. *Journal of Interpersonal Violence, 19,* 468–483.

Fisher, B. S. (1995). Crime and fear on campus. *Annals of the American Academy of Political and Social Science, 539,* 85–101.

Fisher, B. S., Cullen, F. T., & Turner, M. G. (2000). *The sexual victimization of college women.* Washington, D.C.: U.S. Department of Justice.

Fisher, B. S., Sloan, J. J., Cullen, F. T., & Lu, C. (1998). Crime in the ivory tower: The level and sources of student victimization. *Criminology, 36,* 671–710.

Follingstad, D. R., Chahal, J. K., Bush, H. M., Coker, A. L., Li, C. R., Wu, X., Brancato, C., & Carlson, C. R. (2020). A campus climate/violence survey's psychometrics and findings. *Violence against Women.* https://doi.org/10.1177/1077801220969870

Foshee, V. A., Bauman, K. E., Ennett, S. T., Linder, G. F., Benefield, T., & Suchindran, C. (2004). Assessing the long-term effects of the Safe Dates program and a booster in preventing and reducing adolescent dating violence victimization and perpetration. *American Journal of Public Health, 94,* 619–624.

Foster, C., Caravelis, C., & Kopak, A. (2014). National college health assessment measuring negative alcohol-related consequences among college students. *American Journal of Public Health Research, 2,* 1–5.

Fox, J. A., & Savage, J. (2009). Mass murder goes to college: An examination of changes on college campuses following Virginia Tech. *American Behavioral Scientist, 52,* 1465–1485.

Franklin, C. A., Menaker, T. A., & Jin, H. R. (2019). University and community resources for sexual assault survivors: Familiarity with and use of services among college students. *Journal of School Violence, 18,* 1–20.

French, E. (2021). Senate approves updated sexual consent laws. *VTDigger.* https://vtdigger.org/2021/05/13/senate-approves-updated-consent-laws-intercollegiate-sexual-violence-prevention-council/

Fromme, K., Corbin, W. R., & Kruse, M. I. (2008). Behavioral risks during the transition from high school to college. *Developmental Psychology, 44,* 1497–1504.

Garland, D. (2001). *Culture of control.* Oxford: Oxford University Press.

Giambrone, A. (2015). Are college students partying less? *The Atlantic*. https://www.theatlantic.com/education/archive/2015/02/are-college-students-partying-less/385326/

Glass, N. (2012, May 8). Examining the benefits of Greek life. *USA Today*. http://college.usatoday.com/2012/05/08/examining-the-benefits-of-greek-life/

Gross, K., & Fine, A. (1990, February 19). After their daughter is murdered at college, her grieving parents mount a crusade for campus safety. *People, 33*, 113–114.

Harper, S., Maskaly, J., Kirkner, A., & Lorenz, K. (2017). Enhancing title IX due process standards in campus sexual assault adjudication: Considering the roles of distributive, procedural, and restorative justice. *Journal of School Violence, 16*, 302–316.

Hartocollis, A. (2019). New wave of student activism presses colleges on sexual assault. *New York Times*. https://www.nytimes.com/2019/06/08/us/college-protests-dobetter.html

Heaphy, T. J. (2017). *Final report: Independent review of the 2017 protest events in Charlottesville, Virginia*. Hunton & Williams. https://www.huntonak.com/images/content/3/4/v4/34613/final-report-ada-compliant-ready.pdf

Hendrix, S. (2021, March 24). Ohio Sen. Sherrod Brown reintroduces anti-hazing bill in U.S. Senate after BGSU student dies. *Columbus Dispatch*. https://www.dispatch.com/story/news/education/2021/03/24/sen-sherrod-brown-reintroduces-anti-hazing-bill-u-s-senate/6989301002/

Himelein, M. J. (1995). Risk factors for sexual victimization in dating: A longitudinal study of college women. *Psychology of Women Quarterly, 19*, 31–48.

Hines, P. J. (2011). Bracing the armor: Extending rape shield protections to civil proceedings. *Notre Dame Law Review, 86*, 879–904.

Hirsch, J. S., & Khan, S. (2020). *Sexual citizens: A landmark study of sex, power, and assault on campus*. W.W. Norton & Company.

Hoak, A. (2012, August 6). Seven ways to prevent theft on campus. *Market Watch*. Retrieved from: http://www.marketwatch.com/story/7-ways-to-prevent-theft-on-campus-2012-08-06

Hoover, E. (2017, April 9). The arc of her survival. *The Chronicle of Higher Education*. https://www-chronicle-com.proxy.library.vcu.edu/article/the-arc-of-her-survival/

Hoover, N., & Pollard, N. (1999). *National survey: Initiation rites and athletics for NCAA sports teams*. Alfred, New York: Alfred University.

Hyclak, T. (2011). Casinos and campus crime. *Economics Letters, 112*, 31–33.

Jennings, W. G., Gover, A. R., & Pudrzynska, D. (2007). Are institutions of higher learning safe? A descriptive study of campus safety issues and self-reported campus victimization among male and female college students. *Journal of Criminal Justice Education, 18*, 191–208.

Jennings, W. G., Piquero, A. R., & Reingle, J. M. (2012). On the overlap between victimization and offending: A review of the literature. *Aggression and Violent Behavior, 17*, 16–26.

Jones, L. M., Mitchell, K. J., & Walsh, W. A. (2014). *A content analysis of youth Internet safety programs: Are effective prevention strategies being used?* Durham, NH: Crimes Against Children Research Center, University of New Hampshire.

Kaplin, W. A., & Lee, B. A. (2014). Student protests and freedom of speech. In W. A. Kaplin & B. A. Lee (Eds.), *The Law of Higher Education* (5th ed., pp. 602–623). John Wiley & Sons.

Karjane, H. M., Fisher, B. S., & Cullen, F. T. (2002). *Campus sexual assault: How America's institutions of higher education respond*. Washington, D.C.: U.S. Department of Justice.

Kettrey, H. H., & Marx, R. A. (2019). The effects of bystander programs on the prevention of sexual assault across the college years: A systematic review and meta-analysis. *Journal of Youth and Adolescence, 48*, 212–227.

Khalid, A., & Snyder, J. A. (2021). Don't mistake training for education. *Inside Higher Ed.* https://www.insidehighered.com/views/2021/04/29/colleges-should-focus-education-more-training-about-dei-issues-opinion

Kirk-Provencher, K. T., Spillane, N. S., Schick, M. R., Chalmers, S. J., Hawes, C., & Orchowski, L. M. (2021). Sexual and gender minority inclusivity in bystander intervention programs to prevent violence on college campuses: a critical review. *Trauma, Violence, & Abuse.* https://doi.org/10.1177/15248380211021606.

Kirkner, A., Lorenz, K., & Ullman, S. E. (2021). Recommendations for responding to survivors of sexual assault: A qualitative study of survivors and support providers. *Journal of Interpersonal Violence, 36*, 1005–1028.

Know your Title XI. (2015). *Nine things to know about Title XI.* Washington, D.C.: Author.

Kolodner, M. (2020). After George Floyd, students sick of "lip service," want action from colleges over racism. *USA Today.* https://www.usatoday.com/story/news/education/2020/06/20/george-floyd-college-racism/3217298001/

Koss, M. P., & Dinero, T. E. (1989). Discriminant analysis of risk factors for sexual victimization among a national sample of college women. *Journal of Consulting and Clinical Psychology, 57*, 242–250.

Kozlowski, T. (2013, April 16). Emergency phones called into question. *The Signal.* http://www.tcnjsignal.net/2013/04/16/emergency-phones-called-into-question/

Kunst, M., de Groot, G., Meester, J., & van Doorn, J. (2021). The impact of victim impact statements on legal decisions in criminal proceedings: A systematic review of the literature across jurisdictions and decision types. *Aggression and Violent Behavior, 56*, 1–19.

Lee, P. (2018). Student protests and academic freedom in an age of #BlackLivesMatter. *Ohio State Law Journal, 79*, 223–278.

Lewis, J. M., & Hensley, T. R. (2021). *The May 4 shootings at Kent State University: The search for historical accuracy.* Kent State University. https://www.kent.edu/may-4-historical-accuracy

Liedka, R. V., Meehan, A. J., & Lauer, T. W. (2019). CCTV and campus crime: Challenging a technological "fix." *Criminal Justice Policy Review, 30*, 316–338.

Lindsay, T. (2018). Campus free-speech disruptions test our democratic faith. *Forbes.* https://www.forbes.com/sites/tomlindsay/2018/01/18/campus-free-speech-disruptions-test-our-democratic-faith/?sh=62b162a876b5

Loviglio, J. (2003, March 6). U.S. students protest possible Iraq war. *Associated Press.* https://apnews.com/article/8445405cac15891f7e3606f87208d722

MacGreene, D., & Navarro, R. L. (1998). Situation-specific assertiveness in the epidemiology of sexual victimization among university women. *Psychology of Women Quarterly, 22*, 589–604.

Mancini, C. (2020). Mandatory reporting in context: Development, concerns, and best practices. In C. M. Renzetti & D. R. Follingstad (Eds.), *Adjudicating campus sexual misconduct and assault controversies and challenges.* San Diego, CA: Cognella Press.

Mancini, C. (2021). *Sex crime, offenders, and society: A critical look at sexual offending and policy,* 2nd ed. Durham, NC: Carolina Academic Press.

Mancini, C., & Budd, K. M. (2020). Americans' views of efficacy toward campus sexual assault reform. *Journal of School Violence, 19*, 265–276.

Mancini, C., Cook, A. K., Smith, J. C., & McDougle, R. (2020). Packing heat in the classroom: Public support for "armed teacher" policy. *Journal of School Violence, 19*, 610–622.

Marshall, R. (2014). Will it really SaVE you? Analyzing the Campus Sexual Violence Elimination Act. *Legislation and Policy Brief, 6,* 271–293.

McCabe, S. E., Arterberry, B. J., Dickinson, K., Evans-Polce, R. J., Ford, J. A., Ryan, J. E., & Schepis, T. S. (2021). Assessment of changes in alcohol and marijuana abstinence, co-use, and use disorders among U.S. young adults from 2002 to 2018. *JAMA Pediatrics, 175,* 64–72.

McCabe, S. E., Knight, J. R., Teter, C. J., & Wechsler, H. (2005). Non-medical use of prescription stimulants among U.S. college students: Prevalence and correlates from a national survey. *Addiction, 100,* 96–106.

McGrath, S. A., Perumean-Chaney, S. E., & Sloan, J. J. (2014). Property crime on college campuses: A case study using GIS and related tools. *Security Journal, 27,* 263–283.

McPheters, L. R. (1978). Econometric analysis of factors influencing crime on the campus. *Journal of Criminal Justice, 6,* 47–51.

Merianos, A. L., King, K. A., & Vidourek, R. A. (2017). Student perceptions of safety and helpfulness of resources. *American Journal of Health Studies, 32,* 90–101.

Mikkola M., Oksanen A., Kaakinen M., Miller B. L., Savolainen I., Sirola A., Zych I., Paek H. J. (2020). Situational and individual risk factors for cybercrime victimization in a cross-national context. *International Journal of Offender Therapy and Comparative Criminology.* https://doi.org/10.1177/0306624x20981041

Miller, E., Tancredi, D. J., McCauley, H. L., Decker, M. R., Virata, M. C. D., Anderson, H. A., O'Connor, B., & Silverman, J. G. (2013). One-year follow-up of a coach delivered dating violence prevention program: A cluster randomized controlled trial. *American Journal of Preventive Medicine, 45,* 108–112.

Moore, P. J., & Toliver, S. D. (2010). Intraracial dynamics of Black professors' and Black students' communication in traditionally White colleges and universities. *Journal of Black Studies, 40,* 932–945.

Morris, R. G., & Higgins, G. E. (2008). Neutralizing potential and self-reported digital piracy: A multi-theoretical exploration among college undergraduates. *Criminal Justice Review, 34,* 173–195.

Mustaine, E. E., & Tewksbury, R. (1998). Predicting risks of larceny theft victimization: A routine activity analysis using refined lifestyle measures. *Criminology, 36,* 829–858.

Myers, K. (2017). Higher education institutions: Complex and underprepared for active-shooter situations. *Campus Law Enforcement Journal, 47,* 35–37.

Mynatt, C. R., & Allgeier, E. R. (1990). Risk factors, self-attributions, and adjustment problems among victims of sexual coercion. *Journal of Applied Social Psychology, 20,* 130–153.

National Center for Education Statistics. (2020a). *Digest of education statistics (table 329.10).* https://nces.ed.gov/programs/digest/d20/tables/dt20_329.10.asp

National Center for Education Statistics. (2020b). *The condition of education 2020 (NCES 2020–144): Characteristics of postsecondary faculty.* Washington, D.C.: U.S. Department of Justice.

National Center for Victims of Crime. (2015). *Criminal and civil justice.* Washington, D.C.: Author.

National Center on Addiction and Substance Abuse. (2007). *Wasting the best and the brightest: Substance abuse at America's colleges and universities.* New York: Columbia University.

National Conference of State Legislatures. (2019). *Guns on campus: Overview.* Denver, CO: Author.

National Council on Alcoholism and Drug Dependence. (2015). *Underage and college drinking.* New York: Author.

National Institute on Alcohol Abuse and Alcoholism. (2021). College drinking. https://www.niaaa.nih.gov/publications/brochures-and-fact-sheets/college-drinking

Nelson, L. (2015, July 29). Why nearly all colleges have an armed police force. *Vox.* https://www.vox.com/2015/7/29/9069841/university-of-cincinnati-police

New, J. (2014, October 17). The "yes means yes" world. *Inside Higher Ed.* https://www.insidehighered.com/news/2014/10/17/colleges-across-country-adopting-affirmative-consent-sexual-assault-policies

Nobles, M. R., Fox, K. A., Khey, D. N., & Lizotte, A. J. (2010). Community and campus crime: A geospatial examination of the Clery Act. *Crime & Delinquency, 59,* 1131–1156.

Nobles, M. R., Reyns, B. W., Fox, K. A., & Fisher, B. S. (2014). Protection against pursuit: A conceptual and empirical comparison of cyberstalking and stalking victimization among a national sample. *Justice Quarterly, 31,* 986–1014.

Oh, J., & Sundar, S. S. (2016). User engagement with interactive media: A communication perspective. In H. O'Brien & P. Cairns (Eds.), *Why engagement matters: Cross-disciplinary perspectives of user engagement in digital media* (pp. 177–198). Cham, Switzerland: Springer.

O'Hear, M. M. (2007). Plea bargaining and victims: From consultation to guidelines. *Marquette Law Review, 91,* 323–347.

Office for Civil Rights. (2015). *Know your rights: Title IX prohibits sexual harassment and sexual violence where you go to school.* Washington, D.C.: U.S. Department of Education.

Office for Victims of Crime. (2020a). *Victims rights and services.* Washington, D.C.: Office of Justice Programs.

Office for Victims of Crime. (2020b). *What we do.* Washington, D.C.: Office of Justice Programs.

Pedersen, E. R., & LaBrie, J. (2007). Partying before the party: Examining pre-partying behavior among college students. *Journal of American College Health, 56,* 237–245.

Peker, Y. K., Ray, L., Da Silva, S., Gibson, N., & Lamberson, C. (2016). Raising cybersecurity awareness among college students. *Journal of the Colloquium for Information Systems Security Education, 4,* 1–17.

Peterson, J., Sackrison, E., & Polland, A. (2015). Training students to respond to shootings on campus: Is it worth it? *Journal of Threat Assessment and Management, 2,* 127–138.

Pinciotti, C. M., & Orcutt, H. K. (2018). Rape aggression defense: Unique self-efficacy benefits for survivors of sexual trauma. *Violence against Women, 24,* 528–544.

Pizarro, J. M., Zgoba, K. M., & Jennings, W. G. (2011). Assessing the interaction between offender and victim criminal lifestyles and homicide type. *Journal of Criminal Justice, 39,* 367–377.

Plotnikoff, R. C., Costigan, S. A., Kennedy, S. G., Robards, S. L., Germov, J., & Wild, C. (2019). Efficacy of interventions targeting alcohol, drug, and smoking behaviors in university and college students: A review of randomized controlled trials. *Journal of American College Health, 67,* 68–84.

Pugh, B., & Becker, P. (2018). Exploring definitions and prevalence of verbal sexual coercion and its relationship to consent to unwanted sex: Implications for affirmative consent standards on college campuses. *Behavioral Sciences, 8,* 69–97.

Ratti, C. L. (2010). *Student perceptions of campus safety at the University of Mary Washington.* Fredericksburg, VA: University of Mary Washington.

Reaves, B. A. (2015). *Campus law enforcement, 2011–2012.* Washington, D.C.: Bureau of Justice Statistics.

Reilly, K. (2016, August 24). Why banning hard alcohol on college campuses may not be the answer. *Time Magazine*. https://time.com/4463227/stanford-hard-liquor-ban/

Reyns, B. W., & Scherer, H. (2018). Stalking victimization among college students: The role of disability within a lifestyle-routine activity framework. *Crime & Delinquency, 64,* 650–673.

Reyns, B. W., Sween, M., & Randa, R. (2021). College as a risk factor for victimization: Results from the National Crime Victimization Survey. *Victims & Offenders.* https://doi.org/10.1080/15564886.2021.1898506

Rocheleau, M. (2015, January 29). Dartmouth bans hard alcohol, forbids Greek life pledging: Moves target binge drinking, sex assaults. *Boston Globe.* http://www.bostonglobe.com/metro/2015/01/29/dartmouth-college-ban-hard-alcohol-forbid-greek-life-pledging-among-slew-policy-changes/WCxS4OHSLK5hZ5Z7u5E8iN/story.html

Rogers, J. (2018, November 1). How should college leaders respond to campus protests? *Diverse: Issues of Higher Education.* https://diverseeducation.com/article/130873/

Rosenfeld, R., & Messner, S. F. (2013). *Crime and the economy.* Thousand Oaks, CA: Sage.

Rothschild, N. (2020, July 15). Students say they'll sacrifice fun if they can return to campus. *Axios.* https://www.axios.com/college-students-return-campus-poll-fc32654f-39e1-4d69-9e90-f2c54f8fba48.html

Rothman, E., & Silverman, J. (2007). The effect of a college sexual assault prevention program on first-year students' victimization rates. *Journal of American College Health, 55,* 283–290.

Sabina, C., Verdiglione, N., & Zadnik, E. (2017). Campus responses to dating violence and sexual assault: Information from university representatives. *Journal of Aggression, Maltreatment, & Trauma, 26,* 88–102.

Sanburn, J. (2015, January 29). Dartmouth bans hard alcohol on campus for all. *Time Magazine.* http://time.com/3687678/dartmouth-alcohol-ban/

Santelli, J. S., Grilo, S. A., Choo, T. H., Diaz, G., Walsh, K., Wall, M., Hirsch, J. S., Wilson, P. A., Gilbert, L., Khan, S., & Mellins, C.A. (2018). Does sex education before college protect students from sexual assault in college? *PloS One, 13,* e0205951.

Schildkraut, J., Elsass, H. J., & Meredith, K. (2018). Mass shootings and the media: Why all events are not created equal. *Journal of Crime and Justice, 41,* 223–243.

Schmidt, C. (2018). *The sit-ins: Protest and legal change in the civil rights era.* Chicago: University of Chicago Press.

Schroeder, L. P. (2014). Cracks in the ivory tower: How the Campus Sexual Violence Elimination Act can protect students from sexual assault. *Loyola University Chicago Law Journal, 45,* 1195–1243.

Schulenberg, J., Johnston, L., O'Malley, P., Bachman, J., Miech, R., & Patrick, M. (2020). *Monitoring the Future national survey results on drug use, 1975-2019: Volume II, college students and adults ages 19–60.* Ann Arbor, MI: Institute for Social Research, University of Michigan.

Senn, C. Y., Eliasziw, M., Barata, P. C., Thurston, W. E., Newby-Clark, I. R., Radtke, H. L., & Hobden, K. L. (2015). Efficacy of a sexual assault resistance program for university women. *New England Journal of Medicine, 372,* 2326–2335.

Shellenbarger, S. (2005, July 28). Tucking the kids in—in the dorm: Colleges ward off overinvolved parents. *Wall Street Journal.* http://www.wsj.com/articles/SB112250452603298007

Siegel, L. (2018). *Criminology: Theories, patterns, and typologies* (13th ed.). Belmont, CA: Wadsworth/Cengage.

Siegel, L., & Worrall, J. L. (2018). *Introduction to criminal justice* (16th ed.). Belmont, CA: Wadsworth/Cengage.

Sinozich, S., & Langton, L. (2014). *Rape and sexual assault victimization among college-age females, 1995–2013*. Washington, D.C.: Bureau of Justice Statistics.

Skogan, W. G. (1977). Dimensions of the dark figure of unreported crime. *Crime & Delinquency, 23*, 41–50.

Small, M. (2002). *Antiwarriors: The Vietnam War and the battle for America's hearts and minds*. Lanham, MD: Rowman & Littlefield.

Smith, B. G., Krishna, A., & Al-Sinan, R. (2019). Beyond slacktivism: Examining the entanglement between social media engagement, empowerment, and participation in activism. *International Journal of Strategic Communication, 13*, 182–196.

Sokolow, B. (2020, January 15). OCR is about to rock our worlds. *Inside Higher Ed*. https://www.insidehighered.com/views/2020/01/15/how-respond-new-federal-title-ix-regulations-being-published-soon-opinion

Stewart, J. B. (1987). *The prosecutor*. New York: Simon and Schuster.

StopHazing. (2021). States with anti-hazing laws. *StopHazing Consulting*. https://stophazing.org/policy/state-laws

Tenerowicz, L. (2000). Student misconduct at private colleges and universities: A roadmap for fundamental fairness in disciplinary proceedings. *Boston College Law Review, 42*, 653–693.

Thomas, D., & Menasce Horowitz, J. (2020). Support for Black Lives Matter has decreased since June but remains strong among Black Americans. *Pew Research Center*. https://www.pewresearch.org/fact-tank/2020/09/16/support-for-black-lives-matter-has-decreased-since-june-but-remains-strong-among-black-americans/

Thompson, C. (2021, June 28). Family of Adam Oakes pushes to strengthen Virginia hazing laws. *WTVR*. https://www.wtvr.com/news/local-news/family-of-adam-oakes-pushes-to-strengthen-virginia-hazing-laws

Title IX of the United States Education Amendments of 1972, Public Law No. 92-318, 86 Stat. 235 (June 23, 1972), codified at 20 U.S.C. §§ 1681-1688.

Trangenstein, P., Wall, P., & Jernigan, D. (2019). Collateral damage from college drinking: A conceptual framework for alcohol's harms to others among U.S. college students. *Substance Use & Misuse, 54*, 1297–1308.

University of Nevada-Las Vegas. (2021). *How do I file a police report*. https://www.unlv.edu/news-story/how-do-i-file-police-report

University of Tampa. (2021). *Victim advocacy*. https://www.ut.edu/campus-life/student-services/victim-advocacy

Urbina, I. (2009, December 5). Report on Virginia Tech shooting finds notification delays. *New York Times*, p. A1.

U.S. Department of Education. (2014). *Campus security*. Washington, D.C.: Author.

U.S. Department of Education. (2011). *The handbook for campus safety and security reporting*. Washington, D.C.: Author.

U.S. Department of Education. (2020). *Title IX: Fact sheet: Final Title IX regulations*. Washington, D.C.: Author.

U.S. Senate Subcommittee on Financial & Contracting Oversight. (2014). *Sexual violence on campus: How too many institutions of higher education are failing to protect students*. http://www.mccaskill.senate.gov/SurveyReportwithAppendix.pdf

Van Dyke, N. (1998). Hotbeds of activism: Locations of student protest. *Social Problems, 45*, 205–220.

Walsh, K., Sarvet, A. L., Wall, M., Gilbert, L., Santelli, J., Khan, S., Thompson, M. P., Reardon, L., Hirsch, J. S., & Mellins, C. A. (2019). Prevalence and correlates of sexual assault perpetration and ambiguous consent in a representative sample of college students. *Journal of Interpersonal Violence, 36*, 7005–7026.

Wechsler, H., Lee, J. E., Nelson, T. F., & Kuo, M. (2002). Underage college students' drinking behavior, access to alcohol, and the influence of deterrence policies: Findings from the Harvard School of Public Health College Alcohol Study. *Journal of American College Health, 50*, 223–236.

Wechsler, H., Nelson, T. F., Lee, J. E., Seibring, M., Lewis, C., & Keeling, R. P. (2003). Perception and reality: A national evaluation of social norms marketing interventions to reduce college students' heavy alcohol use. *Journal of Studies on Alcohol and Drugs, 64*, 484–494.

Wechsler, H., Seibring, M., Liu, I. C., & Ahl, M. (2004). Colleges respond to student binge drinking: Reducing student demand or limiting access. *Journal of American College Health, 52*, 159–168.

Weiss, K. G., & Dilks, L. M. (2016). Intoxication and crime risk: Contextualizing the effects of "party" routines on recurrent physical and sexual attacks among college students. *Criminal Justice Review, 41*, 173–189.

Welsh, J. W., Shentu, Y., & Sarvey, D. B. (2019). Substance use among college students. *FOCUS, A Journal of the American Psychiatric Association, 17*, 117–127.

Wheatle, K. (2020, March 12). The tradition of student activism influencing higher education policy. *Higher Learning Advocates.* https://higherlearningadvocates.org/2020/03/12/the-tradition-of-student-activism-influencing-higher-education-policy/

Wick, S. E., Nagoshi, C., Basham, R., Jordan, C., Kim, Y. K., Nguyen, A. P., & Lehmann, P. (2017). Patterns of cyber harassment and perpetration among college students in the United States: A test of routine activities theory. *International Journal of Cyber Criminology, 11*, 24–38.

Wolfgang, M. E. (1957). Victim precipitated criminal homicide. *Journal of Criminal Law and Criminology, 48*, 1–11.

Wolfgang, M. E., & Singer, S. I. (1978). Victim categories of crime. *Journal of Criminal Law and Criminology, 69*, 379–394.

Wright, L. A., Zounlome, N. O., & Whiston, S. C. (2020). The effectiveness of male-targeted sexual assault prevention programs: A meta-analysis. *Trauma, Violence, & Abuse, 21*, 859–869.

Yabe, M. (2017). Cost-benefit evaluation: Students', faculty's, and staff's willingness to pay for a campus safety app. *Journal of Criminal Justice Education, 28*, 207–221.

Zapp, D., Buelow, R., Soutiea, L., Berkowitz, A., & DeJong, W . (2021). Exploring the potential campus-level impact of online universal sexual assault prevention education. *Journal of Interpersonal Violence, 36*, 2324–2345.

Author Biography

Christina Mancini, Ph.D., is an Associate Professor at Virginia Commonwealth University's L. Douglas Wilder School of Government and Public Affairs. She received her doctoral degree from Florida State University's College of Criminology and Criminal Justice in 2009. Dr. Mancini has authored or co-authored over 35 peer-reviewed articles examining patterns of sexual offending, law and policy, violent victimization, public opinion, and criminological theory. Her scholarship is featured in highly ranked journals such as *Criminology, Crime & Delinquency, Journal of Research in Crime and Delinquency*, the *Journal of Criminal Law & Criminology*, the *Journal of Criminal Justice*, and other outlets. She is the author of the book *Sex Crime, Offenders, and Society: A Critical Look at Sexual Offending and Policy*, 2nd Edition (Carolina Academic Press, 2021). She currently serves as an editorial advisory board member for several law and policy journals. In 2016, Dr. Mancini, along with colleagues, founded the Sexual Offense Policy and Research (SOPR) Workgroup, a non-profit organization dedicated to improving responses to address sexual violence (http://www.sopresearch.org/).